D0365418

WORLD ECONOMY
AND
WORLD HUNGER:
The Response of the Churches

Robert L. McCan
Associate for Research and Development
Churches' Center for Theology and Public Policy

UNIVERSITY PUBLICATIONS
OF AMERICA
for the
Churches' Center for Theology and Public Policy
4500 Massachusetts Avenue, NW
Washington, DC 20016

TABLE OF CONTENTS

CHAPTER THREE: A CRITICAL REVIEW OF CHURCH-RELATED HUNGER PROGRAMS

CHAPTER FOUR: AN EVALUATION OF THE CHURCHES' RESPONSE -- WITH SUGGESTIONS

FOREWORD

Christian concern about hunger is hardly a New Thing in this generation. What is new since the mid-1970s is the attention which the churches of the United States have given to world hunger as a truly global problem. This book is a serious attempt to evaluate a broad sample of the churches' responses to world hunger.

Basic to this evaluation is one of the official objectives of the Churches' Center for Theology and Public Policy: "To develop humane perspectives on policy issues and processes, with special concern for justice to the poor, the powerless, and the oppressed and for the peace of the whole human family." More particularly, the assumption that poverty is basic in the causation of hunger accounts for the focus of this study on systemic economic issues. Whatever other norms may be appropriate for judging what churches do about hunger, nothing can be more fundamental than effective engagement in the abolition of poverty.

It is our hope, therefore, that this study will serve another of the Center's objectives: "To empower church leaders and groups for competent and credible action in the policy arena by a thorough grounding in research and reflection." There is perhaps no cause more vulnerable to compassionate intentions which lead to irresponsible action than the hunger of poor people. Competent and credible action is the mark of faithful witness which is mature enough to put all good intentions to the test of actually meeting the most basic human needs.

Dr. Robert L. McCan, Associate for Research and Development at the Center, brings broad experience and very special gifts to the execution of this study. He has worked for the United States government in anti-poverty programs at both the domestic and international levels. He has recently completed a book for the International Communication Agency titled An Outline of American Economics. He was the founding president of Dag Hammarskjold College and has served as president of the United Nations Association, Capitol Area Division. He has been a pastor and a politician. It is a privilege to be associated with him and with this study which he has conducted so excellently.

The Center wishes to acknowledge the substantial grant from the United Methodist Board of Church and Society which has made this study possible. We also acknowledge with gratitude the cooperation and professional assistance provided by University Publications of America.

Alan Geyer
Executive Director
Churches' Center for
Theology and Public Policy

PREFACE

This study is directed especially to church executives who are responsible for world hunger programs within their denominations. Others of you who are concerned with justice in the international economic order are invited to join them and see how developing nations can be assisted in their urgent quest in overcoming haunting poverty. You, too, are invited to review the hunger programs of specific denominations and see whether yhou agree with my criteria for evaluating the response of the churches to world hunger and poverty.

Despite their obvious shortcomings, the churches still offer the best hope for society when confronted with complex issues related to the international economic order. A strong sense of compassion and social concern emerge when the love of Jesus comes into contact with the deep needs of suffering humanity.

I have tried to call forth the courage and vision of the prophets, yet I am aware that church leaders are also pastors and partners with the laity who hold widely differing views on global economic issues. Yet we are called by one whose outstretched hands bear the marks of nailprints. Make no mistake, we are challenged to remove all barriers and institute whatever structures are required to provide sufficient daily bread to every person living on planet earth. Anything less is unacceptable to the Christ whom we are called to serve.

My thank to the Board of Church and Society of the United Methodist Church for the grant that made possible this study. I am grateful to Dr. Alan Geyer for his helpful suggestions in planning the study as well as his constructive and critical eye in reviewing a draft of the manuscript. A panel at the Churches' Center for Theology and Public Policy read and commented on parts of the manuscript and made many helpful suggestions following an oral presentation to them.

Finally, my thanks to my wife, Peggy, who gave enthusiastic support support at every turn, edited the manuscript and helped prepare it for publication. The quality of her support is such that I can express it only as pure gift.

                                        Robert L. McCan

CHAPTER ONE

TOWARD THE ELIMINATION OF WORLD HUNGER

...hunger exists in large part because the
continued existence of these poor either serves,
or does not threaten, certain vested economic
and political interests.[1]

By creating and redeeming us through Jesus Christ,
he has given us a love that will not turn aside
from those who lack daily bread.[2]

I. AN OVERVIEW OF HUNGER AND ITS CAUSES

In this eighth decade of the 20th century, the world is polarized
into rich nations and poor nations. Generally, the rich live in the northern
hemisphere and the poor live in the South. The North is overfed and over-
weight, while the South is hungry and malnourished. The North is socially
mobile and lives with the expectation of a better tomorrow; the South, on the
other hand, is rigidly stratified. Most movement in the South is from
country to city, with the resultant destruction of supportive cultural and
family ties and with little short-term improvement in economic opportunity.

The North includes two industrialized countries south of the equator
-- Australia and New Zealand. China, which is basically in the southern
hemisphere, is usually excluded from classification, as it has not joined
with any grouping of countries. Likewise, Eastern European countries choose
not to be included with the North, as their orientation is East-West.

Number and Location of the Malnourished

Of the 4.5 billion people who inhabit planet earth today, 3.3
billion live in the developing world and 1.2 billion live in the North.
Current population growth is at the rate of 70-80 million people per year,
with 86 percent of the increase in the South. ⌊By the year 2000, population
is estimated by the United Nations to be at least six billion, with eight
out of every ten people living in the developing world.[3]⌋

There is no accurate count of how many malnourished people there are
in the world. The Food and Agriculture Organization of the United Nations
(FAO) estimates that in 1975 approximately 450 million people were eating
less than their minimum daily requirements of calories and protein, while
additional large numbers were malnourished for at least a part of each year.

The diets of many other people, even though they have enough to eat, are deficient in essential vitamins and minerals. The most prevalent form of malnutrition is iron deficiency anemia which saps energy and reduces muscular work capacity. Another form, Vitamin A deficiency, blinds 100,000 children annually.[4]

In his 1976 report to the Board of Governors of the World Bank, President Robert McNamara divided nations into "developed," middle-level," and "poorest." He defined the poorest nations as those having per capita annual incomes of $200 per year or less. These poorest nations contain 1.2 billion people, more than one of every four persons on earth. Approximately one of every two persons in these countries is severely malnourished. President McNamara went on to explain what it means to be born into one of these poorest countries as compared to a developed one. Individuals have:

* an infant mortality rate eight times higher,
* a life expectancy one-third lower,
* an adult literacy rate 60 percent less, and
* a nutrition level for one of every two in the population
  below minimum acceptable standards, and for millions of
  infants less protein than is sufficient to permit optimum
  development of the brain.

In the highly significant book North-South: A Program for Survival, the Independent Commission on International Development Issues, chaired by Willy Brandt of West Germany, stated:

> No one knows how many people are undernourished and
> hungry, but much evidence suggests that the number
> could be more than one-fifth of the whole third
> world, or 500-600 million people.[5]

For purposes of this study we shall make a conservative estimate and assume there are 500 million people in the world who are hungry or malnourished. They are the ones who present us daily with "an invisible crisis, a daily tragedy that deprives (these) hundreds of millions the right to realize their genetic potential -- their birthright."[6]

Where do these hungry people live? Four large countries of Asia -- Bangladesh, India, Indonesia and Pakistan -- contain about two-thirds of the world's poor. The others live, for the most part, in other poorest countries. The present United Nations list of what is often termed "the fourth world" includes 29 countries with a population of 258 million. They are found contiguously in two "poverty belts." One extends across the middle of Africa from the Sahara to Lake Nyasa in the south. The other begins with the two Yemens and Afghanistan and stretches eastward across South Asia and into some East Asian countries. Most have fragile tropical environments which have been upset by the growing pressure of people.

These poorest countries are defined as those with a gross national product of $100 per year or less at 1970 prices, and 20 percent or less literacy for persons 15 years of age or older. The economic growth rate of these countries for the past two decades has been less than one percent per year.[7]

Food is NOT the Basic Issue

There is enough food being produced in the world now to provide a high nutritional level for every person. The world is producing every day "two pounds of grain, or more than 3,000 calories, for every man, woman and child on earth." Three thousand calories is about what the average American consumes. This estimate of supply does not take into account many staples such as beans, potatoes, cassava, fresh fruit and vegetables which are grown and consumed locally.[8]

Furthermore, thoughtful specialists believe there can be enough food to provide an adequate diet in the year 2000, even if world population reaches 6.5 billion by that time. But food production will have to nearly double the present amount merely to maintain current levels of consumption. In fact, "the increase in the earth's food-producing capacity over the next three decades would have to equal that achieved from the time agriculture originated to the present." And yet dispassionate scientists believe that such growth in food production is entirely within the realm of the possible. The problem is more complex than that, however, because as nations and individuals raise their standards of living they increase their own food consumption, especially in the form of livestock products. Now the two billion people living in the poor countries consume an average of 400 pounds of grain per person annually, a little more than a pound per day, but middle-level Europeans require a half-ton of grain per year, while the affluent people of the United States each use a ton of grain per year.[9]

Nonetheless, when one considers how technically advanced countries have been able to increase yield per acre, how new strains of grain have revolutionized production through the "Green Revolution," how food can be enriched at low cost by adding protein and vitamins to traditional diets, how water can be piped from one area to another, and how scores of other imaginative and technically feasible plans can be put into effect, there is little doubt but that all the people of the world could be adequately fed in the year 2000. Also, according to FAO, less than 60 percent of the world's cultivable land is now in crop production.

Food production is increasing everywhere except in Africa where production is decreasing gradually while the population is growing by some 2.8 percent annually. This dwindling of food production is taking place while only 20 percent of the potentially arable land in Africa is being cultivated.

If actual past trends were to continue, food production would increase by 2.7 percent annually to some 2.1 billion metric tons of grain by the year 2000, a 40 percent rise above 1978 levels. This amount would probably meet the commercial demand for food, but not the nutritional need. However, in a projection to 1990, FAO concluded that by taking 32 million metric tons of grain per year above commercial demand, all malnourished people of the world could have food stamps equal to those used now in the United States. While this is only two percent of world grain production, that much grain imported to developing countries represents 20 percent of world grain trade.

From this brief survey we can draw two significant conclusions: first, there is now, and there can still be in the year 2000, enough food in the world to provide adequately for every person. Secondly, food distribution is a far more serious problem than food production.

Poverty: The Key Economic Problem

If, by some miracle, food production were to double overnight, most of the malnourished people of the earth would awaken tomorrow still feeling the dull, gnawing pangs of hunger. The 500 million people who live in absolute poverty would still have no money to buy food. With at least one of every eight men, women, and children on the planet suffering malnutrition severe enough "to shorten life, stunt growth, and dull mental ability,"[10] those same people would still be cursed by the same plight -- no money to go to the market and purchase food they need. As the Interreligious Task Force on U.S. Food Policy pointed out:

> Hunger is class specific. It affects most directly
> and most painfully the poor....The problem is cruelly
> simple. When and where food is available, if people
> cannot afford to purchase it, it is simply not
> available to them...if they are hungry because they
> are poor, then we must respond to their poverty.[11]

The Presidential Commission on World Hunger was clear in its conclusion that poverty is the basic cause of world hunger and, therefore, a lasting solution can come only from "rapid, equitable and self-reliant economic growth." For the Commission, the key to breaking the cycle of poverty is to make structural changes within countries and in the international economic order. The Commission said:

> Because hunger and poverty are deeply rooted in
> political and economic relations among and within
> nations, fundamental changes in the patterns of
> landholding, food production, trade and finance
> are needed so that the developing countries can
> break the cycle of hunger, poverty, stagnant
> agricultural productivity, unemployment, high
> birth rates and disease.[12]

Likewise, the Willy Brandt report saw the issue primarily as a skewed international economic order. The report stated:

> In a world as in nations, economic forces left
> entirely to themselves tend to produce growing

inequality. Within nations public policy has to
protect the weaker partners. The time has come to
apply this precept to relations between nations
within the world community.[13]

The Importance of Human Resource Development

For most westerners there is a direct relationship between the notion
of individual worth and the person's contribution to the productive process.
Without work, people cease to be valuable. Yet, lack of employment and low
productivity are characteristic of any underdeveloped economy. Further,
without imposing a western technological mindset on the rural poor of the
world, one can conclude that it is both inefficient and demoralizing to use
extremely primitive methods of farming. Throughout rural Nigeria, for example, one is struck by the sight of women planting corn using short-handled
hoes, dropping one seed at a time into the soil. The corn is pathetic in
quality and yields are extremely low by American standards.

While there are dangers in imposing high technology on developing
cultures, there is no virtue in low productivity. Productivity does not
guarantee food for the poor, but it does determine the "income pie" that is
to be divided; increasing productivity is critical to getting food for the
hungry in much of the developing world. For example, in developing countries, 92 percent of the world's rice is grown with an average yield per
hectare of 1.5 tons per year. In the developed part of the world, 5.5 tons
of rice per year per hectare are grown on soil no better than that used in
the developing world.

Leaders of developing countries are keenly aware of the need to
invest in education, health, and at least low-technology equipment and
skills. For agriculture to become productive and life-enhancing, a basic
ingredient is popular participation through rural development organizations.
Again, human resource development is an essential ingredient.

Literacy is a basic criterion of human resource development in a
technological society. There are still 34 countries where over 80 percent of
the population is illiterate. Nonetheless, the situation is improving rather
dramatically. While only one-third of the adults in developing countries
were literate in 1940, a little over one-half were literate in 1975.[14]

An unending dilemma in poor countries revolves around how much of
very limited resources to spend for human resource development. This expenditure must be weighed against how much to allot for large-scale projects
such as highways, harbors, industrial development, and smaller-scale development such as direct assistance to peasants in rural areas who seek to
increase food production.

While the developing world has a tremendous need for general education, technical skill development, and sophistication in public administration, the United States, at the same time, has the opposite problem. U.S.
colleges, universities and technical institutes are overbuilt. This country

has too many faculty members, too many buildings and too much equipment in relation to the diminishing population of young people seeking education and training. Rather than waste this valuable national resource, America should expand even further the opportunities for education and training which the developing world so desperately needs. At the same time, American schools need to be challenged to develop academic curricula and skill courses specifically designed to meet the needs of persons from developing nations.

Meeting Basic Human Needs Within Countries

There are two sets of structural problems that can be addressed by those who join the struggle to overcome poverty and hunger. One is the inequity caused by unfair structural relationships among nations and the other is the inequity of economic and social structures within nations.

This study places its emphasis on the injustice in the global economic system while recognizing the difference of opinion within the Christian community on this issue. There are at least four reasons for holding this position: (1) the global economic system is the basic structure of the world community that fundamentally affects every nation; (2) the United States is the principal actor and the most serious obstacle to making the changes that a new international economic order requires; (3) when the United States gets its house in order and begins to support a more just global society, it will be in a much stronger moral position to seek changes within other countries; and (4) the total wealth of the world is increased as the world economy grows. From this growth poor nations have better opportunity for a share of wealth, even though not a higher percentage, while the churches work for more just structures to evolve.

Nonetheless, this is not an "either-or", but a "both-and matter." This study endorses efforts by church groups to influence American policy through aid, trade relationships, the World Bank, the International Monetary Fund (IMF), and in other ways to ensure that development within countries of the South is geared to meet basic human needs.[15] For example, it is possible for Ghana to double its export earnings by turning more land into cocoa farms. But if the rich in Ghana team with American multinationals to buy up land, and if they exploit the new tenant farmers so that they remain in abject poverty, and then if foreign exchange earnings from cocoa are used to buy cars and television sets for the new middle and upper classes, the development can hurt rather than help the poor and hungry. American public policy should not support such development at the expense of the very poor.

In reality, the number of countries in the world that are consciously working to create a more just social order is limited.[16] Often those who are involved in international trade and those who govern in developing countries are themselves members of an elite group. They tend consciously or unconsciously to structure national policies in their own self-interest and fail to serve the needs of the very poor. Also, many political leaders owe their success in public life to powerful elitist groups who feel they would be hurt by more just laws and economic policies.

So in every U.S. policy related to development or trade, there should be an awareness and concern for the poor with the question of whether they will be benefitted. But this concern would strike home in the third world with more plausibility if the U.S. practiced what it preached and permitted the structures of the global system to become more equitable.

In summary, changes in the international economic order are not a panacea -- they do not guarantee that malnourishment will end for any particular group of people at a given time. BUT THEY ARE A PRECONDITION. The improvements we seek will not happen on a large scale until the basic restructuring is done in the international economic order.

The Moral/Religious Dimension of World Hunger

It is interesting to note that the Presidential Commission's Report, Overcoming World Hunger: The Challenge Ahead, begins with the question "Why should the United States be concerned?" The first answer given is "Moral Obligation and Responsibility." The report says:

> Moral obligation alone would justify giving
> highest priority to the task of overcoming
> hunger. Even now, millions of human beings
> live on the edge of starvation -- in con-
> ditions of subhuman poverty that, if we think
> about them at all, must fill us with shame and
> horror.... Whether one speaks of human rights
> or basic human needs, the right to food is the
> most basic of all.... The world's major religions
> and philosophical systems share two universal
> values: respect for human dignity and a sense
> of social justice. Hunger is the ultimate
> affront to both.[17]

Robert McNamara, President of the World Bank, saw the moral issue clearly when he said:

> Social justice is not simply an abstract ideal.
> It is a sensible way of making life more liv-
> able for everyone. Thus, for the developed
> nations to do more to assist the developing
> countries is not merely the right thing to do,
> it is also increasingly the economically
> advantageous thing to do.[18]

Both the President's Commission on World Hunger and North-South, conclude that malnutrition and absolute poverty could be largely overcome by the year 2000. Continued malnourishment is a moral problem for which we are all responsible when the world has the power to eliminate it. The President's Commission said it well:

> The outcome of the war on hunger by the year
> 2000 and beyond will not be determined

primarily by forces beyond human control,
but rather by decisions and actions well within
the capability of nations working individually
and together.[19]

North-South put the outcome in political terms, but set it in the
concept of social justice:

> ...the principal motives for our proposals
> are human solidarity and a commitment to
> international social justice....The extent
> to which the international system will be
> made more equitable is essentially a matter
> for political decision. We are looking for
> a world based less on power and status, more
> on justice and contract; less discretionary,
> more governed by fair and open rules.[20]

Now let us look briefly at the concept of justice in the international political economy from the perspective of the Bible.

If a poll were taken among church people in North America on why a
half-billion people of the world are malnourished and live in abject poverty,
the major causes might be listed as "underdevelopment" or "lazy" or "racial
or national inferiority." If one goes to the Bible for an answer for why
people are poor, there are a few scattered references to factors such as
laziness, drunkenness and other assorted individual failings. But if one
looks under "oppress" or "oppression" in a concordance, he/she will find 15
root Hebrew words and two Greek words, occurring more than 300 times. In the
Bible there are 122 texts in which oppression is indicated as the cause of
poverty.

The Exodus played a central role in the theology of the Old Testament, comparable to that of the cross in the New Testament. It was in the
Exodus that a people God recognized as oppressed won their liberation. "Let
my people go" were God's words to Pharoah through Moses.

Beginning with Solomon, Israel felt the brunt of internal oppression
from rulers. From this time forth, the prophets spoke of justice within
their social order by denouncing those with power who took advantage of the
poor.

Thus Tom Hanks translates Psalm 72:2-4:

> May he govern your people with justice,
> And your oppressed-poor (ani) with just
> judgments...May he vindicate the oppressed-
> poor of the people, May he save-liberate
> the sons of the needy, And crush the
> oppressor (ashaq).[21]

This author put the implications of the Biblical perspective squarely when he wrote:

> First, in our approach to the poor, whether
> in our own slums or in the third world nations,
> we need to stop justifying our privileges and
> start trying to discover and denounce the
> mechanisms of oppression that make and keep
> people poor. The Biblical prophets were
> geniuses at this. We need to enter into
> the depths of their social analysis and not
> content ourselves with the discovery of
> occasional messianic proof texts.[22]

Justice in the Old Testament is related to one's material security within the context of the community of Israel. Usually it is understood as security in title to one's productive land, but it also represents protection of the economic well-being of vulnerable people, such as widows and orphans and non-property people, including foreigners. "Justice is presented as the condemnation of those who take advantage of the material weakness of the powerless and as a stern admonition of the community not to follow this."

In Christianity, the basis of the moral claim lies in the extent to which inequalities place burdens upon loving human relationships. The basic selfishness in human relationships is termed "sinful" and Christ came to overcome our sin.[23]

A Christian definition of justice begins with the right of persons to provision of their basic needs and the dignity which comes from participating in their common destiny. Exploitation is seen in the New Testament not only as damaging to people but also as a way of wounding God. The critical test of any economic or political system, including the global political economy, is whether it builds or destroys justice in the context of the caring world community. Feeding the hungry on an emergency basis is necessary, but it is an extremely inadequate response to a fundamental theological reality: God's love and care for all hungry and poor, and His overwhelming passion for justice in global society.

Justice in the international economic order is an issue for all world religions because they, with Christianity, are committed to feeding the hungry and bringing God's blessings to the poor. For this to occur in our day, a moral awakening is needed within the churches, within other religions, and in secular societies that will lead to a concerted lobby to influence systemic structures and underlying causes of global poverty.

II. AMERICAN POLICY AND THE NEW INTERNATIONAL ECONOMIC ORDER

The apostle Paul spoke of many members of one body to draw an analogy between the human body and its parts and the various members that comprise

the church. A similar analogy could be drawn today between the human body
and the global community. It, too, is now "one body." The health of the
global community is vital to the health of any member; likewise, healthy
individual nations are necessary if the whole body is to be strong and
prosperous. The Presidential Commission put it this way:

> Since it is increasingly clear that both the
> actors and the issues involved have become
> highly interdependent, our most immediate
> observation is that today, more than ever,
> the economic prospects of poor nations and
> poor people are intimately bound up with
> the evolution of the international economy
> as a whole.[24]

An appeal can be made to Christians in terms of caring for the
entire human family as children of a loving God, or Christians can join
with others in appealing to enlightened self-interest. For the body to be
healthy, all the members must be functioning properly; illness in one part
of the body will spread quickly to those parts that are well.

It then becomes a matter of enlightened self-interest and/or Christian compassion to protect the weak. It is not the rich making sacrifices
for the poor. A significant proportion of jobs in the North today depend
upon trade with the South. The opportunity for even greater prosperity in
the North is increased as the South becomes wealthy enough to buy Northern
products. The achievement of economic growth in one country depends increasingly, therefore, on the performance of others. If this is true, it is
important both to give the weak the opportunity to become stronger and to
build a more healthy world economy.

Importance of a Healthy Global Economy

Even so, the one greatest boon to poor nations is a healthy world
economy that is growing and that experiences an easing of inflationary
pressure. In 1979 the World Bank prepared scenarios based on high-growth
and low-growth and sought to measure the impact of each on the poorest people
of the world. Both projections assumed that no major changes will occur in
the distribution of income among or within nations.

Under the high growth scenario there is a strong expansion of world
trade, permitting developing countries to export a large amount of manufactured goods as well as commodities. Prosperity in the developed nations
would, it was assumed, trigger a higher level of development assistance, so
important for the economic growth of the poorest developing nations.

The low-income scenario assumed that developed nations will recover
slowly from their poor economic performance of the 1970s and that the growth
of world trade will lag, with resulting high unemployment, lower profits and
increased protectionism in trade. At the same time, developing nations will
be able to export less at reasonable prices, and growth in the third world
will be slowed.

Given these two sets of projections, the book, North-South concluded that with the optimistic scenario, 470 million people will still be in absolute poverty in 2000: 340 million people in the low-income developing nations and 130 million in the middle-income nations. The low-growth scenario leaves 710 million of the world's people in absolute poverty in the year 2000: 520 million in the poorest nations and 190 million in the middle-income nations.

The Presidential Commission concluded from this study that: (1) the rate of economic growth for the next twenty years makes a tremendous difference between better living conditions or continued misery for millions of people; and (2) even with the most favorable projection, there will be vast numbers of human beings in poverty in the year 2000.[25]

Based on these conclusions, whether 240 million people remain in abject poverty depends on the general health of the world economy. But even with a healthy economy, it is clear that additional steps will have to be taken to eliminate hunger as a scourge on the world's people. A "Basic Human Needs" approach is necessary -- one that targets economic growth and discreetly chooses development projects for the poorest people.

Of course, the United States cannot create the positive vision of a world without hunger by itself. However, as the world's leader, this nation can set an example as it negotiates trade terms, deals with debt burdens, discourages armaments that take food from the mouths of the poor, influences the policies of international lending agencies, and designs our own aid programs. The most important consideration is acceptance of the need for a new international economic order and a mindset that is willing to negotiate the changes that are required.

Demands for a New International Economic Order

When John Wesley preached to England's poor in the late 18th century, he encountered countless persons who worked hard to better their lot, but were trapped by an industrial system geared to long hours and low wages. It was true that the churches were able to enlist some enlightened industrialists to provide emergency help as charity for the poorest. But John Wesley voiced the frustration of his constituents as well as his own when he cried, "Damn your charity, we want justice!"

What John Wesley saw then, we need to perceive now. The structures of the world economic order are out of balance, favoring rich and powerful nations at the expense of poor, weak ones. To revamp these structures is, in the long run, far more important than providing relief, localized economic aid, or some form of charity.

The basic purpose of the study headed by Willy Brandt of West Germany was to deal with this problem. The Commission stated:

> Most people know that the existing system of
> international institutions was established
> at the end of the Second World War, thirty-

> five years ago, and that the South --
> mostly as latecomers on the international
> scene -- faces numerous disadvantages which
> need fundamental correction. Hence the
> demand for a new international economic
> order.[26]

The sense of common purpose and the recognition of strength through unity began among poor nations in the 1960s. The United Nations Conference on Trade and Development (UNCTAD) in Geneva in 1964 and at Santiago in 1968 were watershed experiences. Both left the South reeling with the realization that they did not have the power to change the economic structures in ways that would provide them with opportunity for economic growth.

The 1970s will be remembered in history both as the era when global interdependence was recognized as an inescapable reality and as the time when a coalition of developing nations emerged, claiming the right to restructure the international economic order. The coalition, commonly called "The Group of 77," now numbers more than 100 nations. They are the "third and fourth world" component of the North-South split. These nations of the South are very diverse in location, type of government and economic needs but they are united by a keen sense of grievance against the industrialized nations and a common desire to restructure the international economic order.

Although the South saw the need for solidarity in the 1960s, it was not until 1973-74 that the dramatic success of the Organization of Petroleum Exporting Countries (OPEC) raised the hopes of these third world nations that something concrete could be done for them. After OPEC's success, they envisioned other cartels being formed which would raise commodity prices, as OPEC had done with oil. As the Dag Hammarskjold Foundation Report noted:

> this decision by the oil exporting countries
> had put an end to an era which had begun with
> what the West calls the "great discoveries."
> For the first time since Vasco deGama, mastery
> over a fundamental decision in a crucial area
> of economic policy of the centre countries
> escaped their group as certain peripheral
> countries wrested it from them.[27]

Special Sessions of the UN on the NIEO

The early history of the drive for restructuring the international economy is instructive. In September 1974, the United Nations called the sixth special session of the General Assembly. Its purpose was to lay the groundwork for a New International Economic Order (NIEO). The Group of 77 was strident and the session was stormy, with the United States and other developed nations resisting the demands of the South.

From the session came a non-binding Charter on "The Economic Rights and Duties of States," which was written primarily by Luis Echeverria Alvarez, President of Mexico. The Charter was approved by a margin of 120 to six, with ten abstentions. But the highly industrialized nations, whose support was crucial to achieving the goals, either abstained or voted against it.

The document affirmed the sovereignty of every state over its wealth, resources, and economic activity. It recognized the right of each nation to control foreign investments in accordance with its own laws and to supervise multinational corporations within its boundaries. Another provision, strenuously resisted by most industrialized nations of the North, recognized the right of southern countries to expropriate foreign property without guaranteeing equitable compensation. The controversial document also provided that trade should be guided by principles of mutual advantage, meaning that export prices of commodities should be adjusted for inflation based on the price of manufactured goods imported into their countries. Finally, the document claimed for the South the right to organize commodity cartels.

After the sixth special session but prior to the seventh, which was called for the following autumn, a conference of 104 developing nations met in Algiers in February 1975. The goal was to devise a program that would raise the South's share of the world economy from seven percent to 25 percent by the year 2000. To reach this goal, they would have to grow at the rate of eight percent a year. How could this be achieved? Answers included establishing cartels to sell their raw materials at much higher prices, nationalization of foreign industries (compensation unspecified), and the transfer of basic industries that are labor intensive from rich to poor countries.

In the fall of 1975, at the seventh special session of the General Assembly, the mood was more conciliatory. The purpose of the session was to consider "Development and International Economic Cooperation." At the conclusion of the session a consensus resolution called for changes that would benefit the South in seven areas: (1) international trade, (2) money and finance, (3) science and technology, (4) industrialization, (5) food and agriculture, (6) cooperation among developing nations, and (7) restructuring of the United Nations system. While everyone agreed in principle, the North stated that implementation would take a long time.

The first step toward implementation of these moderate principles was UNCTAD IV, the Fourth United Nations Conference on Trade and Development which met in Nairobi in May 1976. The priority issue was to set stable prices for commodities sold by the South. The Group of 77 sought an integrated program to deal with unstable prices of raw materials and proposed a "common fund" of $6 billion that would smooth out the highs and lows in price swings. The proposal would have created a fund to purchase reserve commodities when prices were low and to sell from reserves when prices became high because of shortages. The proposals were not acceptable to the United States and other industrial nations, partly because the U.S. did not wish to lump together all commodities with varying degrees of strategic importance and abundance. The North did agree to hold individual conferences to negotiate on each of a long list of commodities.

An UNCTAD IV report to the General Assembly of the UN stated that the most significant features of the negotiations were "on the one hand, the manifestation of the increased bargaining power of the third world, and on the other hand, the wide spectrum of positions adopted by the various developed market economy countries...."

On September 15, 1980, the Eleventh Special Session, building on the sixth and seventh sessions, was designed to push forward the long-stalemated negotiations on a new international economic order. "Yet after nearly six years, the only breakthrough on NIEO goals came in June of this year when agreement was reached on the establishment of a Common Fund to help stabilize and diversify developing countries' export earnings."[28]

The Eleventh Special Session made excruciatingly slow progress toward the new order:

> The United States, which had promised to
> participate "constructively" in a new round
> of global economic negotiations, has started
> off playing the role of the die-hard defender
> of the old order and spoiler of initial efforts
> to get a dialogue underway between the world's
> rich and poor nations.[29]

The Special Session did reach consensus on a new "International Development Strategy" (IDS) for the Third Development Decade. Although it is non-binding, the IDS maps out a strategy for rich and poor nations in the areas of trade, aid, industrialization, agricultural development, disarmament, energy, and other issues.

Attitudes of the Reagan Administration

This brings the account of the saga to the time of the Reagan Administration. At the seventh annual economic summit of leading western nations and Japan held at Ottawa, Canada on July 19-20, 1981, one section of the communique was on North-South relations. The U.S. policy of viewing such issues primarily in terms of East-West was rejected by the other leaders. Under pressure Mr. Reagan accepted the concept of interdependence, a commitment to increase aid, and a reference to work for a "mutually acceptable process of global negotiations." Many at the United Nations and from the other governments were heartened by the U.S. acceptance of this compromise language.

The next step in deciding the process of global negotiations is a meeting to be held at the seaside resort of Cancun, Mexico on October 22-23, 1981. The meeting is called to discuss the implications of the prestigious Brandt report on North-South relations. On August 2, the foreign ministers of the 22 nations met to design the agenda and set forth ground rules in preparation for the coming of heads of state from 14 developing and 8 developed nations.

U.S. Secretary of State Alexander Haig represented the United States in the preparatory meeting. He reported upon his return that he was "very pleased" and saw this as "a historic opportunity for a new beginning" of the North-South dialogue. When pressed by reporters, he indicated that he was pleased because there would be no set agenda, no final conclusions and only 12 hours of discussion time, with each of 22 leaders having only one half-hour to cover all topics. The foreign ministers rejected a motion by Algeria that the proposed "global negotiations" be placed on the agenda. Topics which heads of state are invited to address were to be food security and agricultural development; commodities, trade and industrialization; energy; and monetary and financial issues.[30]

An article in the New York Times, appearing in August 1981, reports an interview with Myer Rashish, the Undersecretary of State for Economic Affairs on the Reagan Administration's position on North-South relationships. Mr. Reagan is opposed to shifting billions of dollars of wealth from the North to the South. The hope for the South is in creation of its own new wealth. According to Mr. Rashish, third world proposals are "instruments for getting resources out of the rich for the so-called poor." He seemed to dismiss the claims of the South by describing them simply as "an essay in distributive justice and equality."

Mr. Rashish rejected all the demands of the South for lower trade barriers, higher prices for their products, increases in foreign aid, and the reshaping of the International Monetary Fund. He described all of these demands as impractical or inefficient.

As principal architect of the Reagan Administration's foreign economic policy, Mr. Rashish was skeptical of the process as well as the substance of the North-South dialogue. The United Nations, in his judgment, is not an appropriate forum. In his view, the United Nations "may prove a useful basis for certain purposes but the global negotiation has not proved useful." When asked about the U.S. attendance at Cancun, he felt those who pinned hopes on a change of U.S. attitudes have been misled. America, he said, is willing to discuss but not to negotiate.[31]

> Our position at Cancun is fully consistent with
> the philosophy of this Administration from its
> beginning...enterprise and the allocation of
> resources through free markets....Our philo-
> sophy does not stop at the waterfront."

Finally, in an address to a United Nations Conference, the new Assistant Secretary of State for International Organization, Elliott Abrams, said when other nations expressed dismay at the hardened American position:

> I don't want to leave you with the taste of
> ashes in your mouth about the Reagan Admin-
> istration or about our attitude toward the

> United Nations....We are committed to making
> the system work on those things that can
> benefit global stability and economic devel-
> opment. The International Conference on
> African refugees in Geneva in April provides
> an example of the kind of role the Reagan
> Administration will pursue.[32]

Now let us review specific negotiations since 1974 and get some idea
of their significance in redressing the imbalance between North and South.[33]

III. U.S. ECONOMIC POLICIES: HOW TO BENEFIT POOR NATIONS

A key issue in building the new international economic order is how
to provide further access for the South's manufactured goods into northern
markets. Many persons perceive the issue simply as one of competition of
third world goods with American workers who lose their jobs because of imports.
The debate rages on about the merits of free trade, but generally workers in
the United States benefit more in the long term through free trade in that
more are employed in exports than lose their jobs from imports; exports could
not be sold abroad unless we also imported products. Further, the American
consumer benefits from lower prices of products they purchase. Finally, the
loss of jobs in the North has been small in relation to total unemployment.
It does have the greatest impact on unskilled workers who find it hardest to
get other employment. The challenge in the United States is to cope with the
difficulties of adjustment in this country so that world trade can expand.
The challenge to the South is to expand expertise and technical capacity to
respond positively to trade opportunities created by improved access to
markets in the North.

The Reagan Administration believes that free trade should be the
policy of the United States in international economics because market forces
should control the economic system. However, in any administration during
times of economic recession there is pressure to protect American workers
more than American consumers. Management and employees join forces to pro-
test the cheaper import of their product and put pressure on government to
provide protection. As a result, higher prices are passed along to consumers. But since no particular group is hurt specifically, the public tends
to pay without any great outcry.

One of the first programs to be curtailed in the austerity drive of
the new administration was a law enacted during the Carter administration
to assist workers who needed to relocate because of loss employment due to
imports.

As manufacturing shifts to developing countries it is important,
also, to encourage the establishment of minimum wages and safe working conditions there. The International Labor Organization has taken this as an
important agenda item; its efforts should be supported.

President Francois Mitterrand of France put trade with the South positively in opening a United Nations conference which was called to organize aid to 31 countries designated as the poorest in the world. He declared: "Helping the Third World is helping yourself pull out of the (economic) crisis. Who still dreams of getting developed economies on the move again in a lasting way without the help of new markets, new partners, new worlds to work with, make exchanges with and speak with equal to equal?"[34]

Processing Commodities in the Third World

Most third world earnings come from commodities -- 57 percent in 1978, or 81 percent if oil is included. Commodities contribute as much as 50-60 percent of the gross national product of many countries. One major problem is that developing countries have little opportunity to participate in the processing, manufacturing, marketing and distribution of their commodities.

When developing countries sell their raw materials they tend to get about 25 percent of final consumer prices. Hence, the real opportunity for profit comes by using their own raw materials and making them into semi-finished or finished products and then selling abroad. UNCTAD estimates that in 1975 the semi-processing of raw materials would have added earnings of about $27 billion for the year, more than one and one-half times what these commodities actually earned.[35]

But developed nations, including the United States, put a tariff on semi-processed materials, and even higher duties on most manufactured goods. For example, the U.S. puts a tariff of nearly 15 percent on milled rice.

The problem is compounded by higher freight rates for semi-processed goods than for raw materials. For export to U.S. markets, freight rates for semi-processed goods were three times as high on rubber exported from Malaysia and twice as high for leather from India or wood from Brazil than for unprocessed raw materials.

Nonetheless, export of manufactured goods from third world countries is increasing. In 1955 they made up only 10 percent of non-fuel exports; in 1965 they were 20 percent and in 1975 they passed 40 percent. However, most of these exports come from only a few countries; eight of them account for 78 percent of the increase in exports. The need now is to include many additional nations in this export community.

Increasingly, the South is selling to other southern nations. In 1976, 22 percent of the South's total exports and 32 percent of its manufactured exports went to other countries in the South. The Soviet Union takes about 6 percent of exports from southern countries. Nonetheless, the real opportunity for growth in southern export of manufactured goods must come from the non-Communist industrialized North. This will require a revolution in employment patterns and a new division of labor in a dynamic process calling for continuous adaptation. Employment in many traditional sectors in the North will diminish as goods from the South are accommodated.

Tariff Reductions and Import Quotas

During the first half of the 1970s, the industrial countries gradually reduced their barriers to trade in manufactured goods, mostly through the successive rounds of multilateral trade negotiations. Total exports from third world countries grew at the rate of 18 percent annually between 1970 and 1976, but at that time the North began to put up barriers again, mostly in the form of quotas. IMPORTS FROM THE SOUTH MET MORE AND HIGHER BARRIERS THAN THOSE FROM MORE INDUSTRIAL COUNTRIES. (Even the threat of restrictions creates an unfavorable climate for the development of manufacturing in the South.)

The balance of trade in manufactured and semi-manufactured goods is highly skewed in favor of the North. In 1978, total imports from the South were $32 billion compared to trade in the opposite direction of $125 billion!

The developing countries have been highly dissatisfied with the Multinational Trade Negotiations of the General Agreement on Tariffs and Trade (GATT), commonly known as the Tokyo Round, despite some acknowledged gains. There will be a liberalization on imports of from 25 to 33 percent over ten years, with the understanding that the U.S. and other industrialized nations can impose emergency restrictions when necessary. And there has been an agreement on new rules for nations in dealing with each other, such as provision for notification, consultation, dispute settlement and surveillance to see that agreements are actually honored.

The Tokyo Round has recognized that preferential treatment of developing countries should be accepted as a permanent practice rather than as a temporary exception. Thus, there is an immediate need to negotiate new policies of preferential treatment to developing countries. However, with the outlook of the present Administration in the United States, the prospects do not appear to be bright.

Two global organizations deal with world trade policies: UNCTAD has universal membership and has become a principal forum for debate and negotiations about change in the international economic system. At the same time, some developing countries are joining GATT with the hope that they can influence its policies. But most feel that GATT is so controlled by the industrialized nations that there is little chance for real change. The Brandt Commission suggested the need for a new trading organization that would encompass the function of both GATT and UNCTAD. Through whatever organization, one of the major instruments for eliminating hunger on a global scale is to restructure the trading system to ensure fairer treatment for the poor nations of the South.

Stable Prices and Fair Terms Through Commodity Agreements

The prices for many commodities are unstable and this leads to unstable income for commodity producers. Very often the developing nation has only one, or perhaps two, major commodities for export. For example, in Zambia, 94 percent of export earnings is from copper; in Gambia, 85 percent is from ground-nuts or ground-nut oil. In Cuba, 84 percent is from sugar.

The impact caused by the fluctuation of commodity prices on development planning and the achievement of growth, even when planning has been effective, is illustrated in the African country of Niger. The seven-year-old military government in Niger set a goal of self-sufficiency in food and an end to mass starvation in the aftermath of the Sahelian drought. Since 1974, Niger has plowed its meager resources and its foreign aid into increased production of staple grains, with the result that production has exceeded the 2.7 percent population growth rate.

Last year Niger's peasants produced 1.7 million tons of grain, mostly sorghum and millet, or 200,000 tons more than the country used. A spokesman stated, "Each year we are getting increases and the farmers are building up their stocks.... We are a proud people."

This growth in food production has been financed in large part by export of uranium from the northern desert region. Exports doubled to 400,000 tons a year in the past two years, with much of the earnings going toward increased food production. However, Niger's leaders are now worried because the price of uranium has dropped from $46 per pound last year to the current price of $32 per pound, and 75 percent of Niger's revenue is from uranium.[36]

The concept of how to stabilize commodities is rather simple: during times of overproduction an internationally controlled body of the United Nations will purchase the surplus and place it in storage. Through this process prices are supported at a reasonable level. Then, during times of great demand when supply is short, these commodities are gradually released, again keeping the price stable and preventing inflation.

One problem for the United States has been its doctrinaire belief that the marketplace should be free and unregulated. Another difficulty for getting agreement is that when prices are falling, consumer nations lose interest, while when they are going up, producers do not want to negotiate.

The Overseas Development Council Study of 1977 indicated the United States would benefit more from such a system than would the nations of the South. On specific commodities, between 1963 and 1973, developing nations would have benefitted by $5 billion through such agreements and the United States would have saved $15 billion in inflation costs. Yet poor nations would have had the basis for rational planning for development, being able to better predict their income.

The South is in the same bind that the American farmer experienced for a long period of this country's history. The populist movement of the early 1900s, culminating in New Deal legislation in the 1930s and a system of parity in the years following, was the American way of dealing with inequity toward farmers. Agriculture products of grain or livestock were priced too low for farmers to afford the higher cost of manufactured products. Parity is a method of tying farmers' costs to farmers' incomes.

The nations of the South find themselves in precisely this bind now in the world economy. Much of their present debt burden is due to the low price they get for unprocessed commodities they export, as compared with the ever escalating cost of goods and services they must import.

In 1976 at the UNCTAD meeting in Nairobi, nations agreed to an Integrated Programme for Commodities which provided for a Common Fund as well as International Commodity Agreements. The Common Fund has two windows: the first will finance buffer stocks and the second other investments which help in production, processing and marketing of commodities. In March 1979, agreement was reached on the principal elements of the Common Fund, but only $400 million has been made available as compared to the original Nairobi agreement in which $1 billion was to be pledged to start the fund.[37]

We noted earlier the demands of the Group of 77 for price stabilization agreements. The United States has led in opposing negotiations on commodity support systems in general, but has agreed to negotiations on some individual commodities. Under UNCTAD, four agreements have now come into existence -- sugar, tin, coffee, and rubber.

Recently, Mr. Myer Rashish, speaking for President Reagan, accepted commodity stabilization in the areas where negotiations are completed, but said such agreements are possible only on items where there is a balance of interest between consumers and producers, and concluded, "This list has been exhausted." Instead of new pacts, Mr. Rashish suggested that poor countries borrow from the IMF when commodity prices drop, and urged them to "respond to market signals cutting output when prices fall."[38]

International Monetary Fund Policies

The IMF is probably the most powerful international economic institution in the world, with direct control over the internal policies of most of the poorest nations of the world. Therefore, if the world's poorest people are to escape hunger, the policies and actions of the IMF must be directed to that goal. The IMF is recognized by both official aid agencies and private commercial banks as the institution that must approve external loans for developing countries. For poor nations to borrow necessary funds, they must agree to internal policies dictated by the Fund.

Final decisions on the conditions for loans rest with the IMF's 21 Executive Directors, representing member governments. The five richest countries plus Saudi Arabia each have their own Executive Director; other countries share an Executive Director. Voting strength is in proportion to the country's assigned quota. As the nation with the largest economy, the United States has 20 percent of the voting strength. On the other hand, the 37 low-income African countries share two Executive Directors and have a cumulative vote of less than six percent of the IMF's total.

Dramatic increases in oil prices since 1974, increases in the cost of manufactured goods, and higher food prices have all contributed to radically higher import costs for developing countries. At the same time, as we have noted, prices received by less developed countries for their exports -- chiefly commodities and raw materials -- have been declining in relation to their purchasing power. As a result, the third world debt reached the astounding total of $358 billion by the end of 1980.

The exact terms of IMF loan agreements with debtor nations are negotiated on an individual basis. However, because they are desperate for these loans, countries feel they must negotiate agreements. Usually the IMF requires that the country take such steps as:

* devalue its currency to boost exports and limit imports;
* control the rate of expansion of the money supply to dampen inflation;
* reduce government spending, especially for human services;
* impose wage controls, while eliminating price controls;
* raise interest rates in order to encourage savings;
* increase taxes;
* reduce or dismantle barriers to foreign private investment and to free trade.

Usually the terms of the agreement are negotiated by the elite of the country, and the conditions that result favor that elite at the expense of the poor. By controlling the money supply, borrowing by small businesses or groups such as rural cooperatives becomes more difficult. Wage controls without price controls hurt the laboring people but help those who manufacture or employ large numbers of people. Cutbacks in spending for essential human services (housing, education, health care) hit the poor the hardest. Emphasis on exports often diverts land from crops that feed local people to different crops that benefit buyers in developed countries.

In August 1979 an article appeared in the New York Times providing details of the human costs for Peru of IMF imposed policies:

In the last four years, the worker's real buying
power has been cut in half. Only 45 percent of
the 5.2 million in the workforce have stable work.
The price of bread has jumped 1,000 percent. Per
capita calorie and protein intake are but two-
thirds of those listed by the Food and Agriculture
Organization as the vital minimum.... Nationally,
the number of babies who die before they learn to
walk has jumped some 30 percent, to 109 per 1,000.
That translates into an additional 13,000 infant
deaths a year. No one seems to notice. Children
have a way of dying quietly. It's a massacre of
the innocents.

The World Bank is moving toward a policy of meeting basic human needs
through its loans. Yet this sister organization has gone in the other direction, with "monetarist" policies that result in increased human suffering and
a widening gap between the rich and poor.[39]

In recent months because of mounting criticism, the IMF has begun to
modify its policies and ease the burdens placed on the poor within nations.
Some basic changes in programs for helping the poorest people are still
needed for the IMF. They include: (1) revising policies required for a
nation to get a loan so that basic human needs are protected; (2) increasing
voting strength of third world governments within the IMF; (3) easing debt
burdens through a longer term for repayment, or even better, a one-time debt
forgiveness as a mechanism of aid; (4) continuing the sale of gold reserves
and using the money for development; (5) continuing the expansion of funds
available for loans to countries in financial distress.[40]

An important step was taken with the establishment of the "Special
Trust Fund" of the IMF, which was financed initially through the sale of IMF
gold. It set a precedent for imaginative assistance to poorest countries.
Since gold is no longer the international medium of exchange, holdings of
the IMF were no longer needed.[41] According to a Brookings study:

The Jamaica accord stipulates that one-sixth of
the IMF's gold be sold at the low official price
to Fund members in proportion to their quotas, and
one-sixth be sold by the IMF in the private market
over a four-year period, with the profits, or the
difference between the realized price and the
official price of $42 per ounce, going directly
or indirectly to the developing countries....
The Fund should be authorized to sell the
remaining two-thirds of its gold in an orderly
way and use the proceeds entirely for the
benefit of developing countries, particularly
the poorest countries among them.

U.S. Participation in Other United Nations Programs

Three programs of the United Nations which contribute directly toward overcoming world hunger are the Food and Agriculture Organization (FAO), the UN High Commissioner for Refugees (UNHCR), and the United Nations Development Program (UNDP). These organizations are significant because they have a global perspective and because their membership includes those who are recipients as well as donors. They are, for the same reasons, often cumbersome and difficult to manage.

(a) A System of World Grain Reserves

FAO programs are designed to raise nutrition levels and living standards, and improve food production and distribution. FAO carries out field projects for food production and distribution, processing and storage, conducts training programs, and monitors world food supply. Perhaps the program with the greatest potential impact is the World Food Security Program which is concerned with production, storage and availability of grain. In the poorest nations, grain accounts for well over half of total calorie intake. It is important, therefore, that grain not only be available but that prices be kept stable so the poor can purchase the maximum amount of food.

In the recent past, world production shortfalls of 10 percent have been linked to price increases for wheat and rice of 200 percent or more. In times of such shortage, nations with more wealth can easily draw the supply away from poor nations where there is no margin between a minimum daily intake and severe malnutrition. The most effective way to prevent such shortfalls among those who need food the most is to encourage food self-sufficiency in each nation. However, additional steps will always need to be taken.

Grain reserves are vital to feeding hungry people in times of shortage and in keeping a moderate and stable price for food. An effective grain reserve must provide for location of grain in strategic places based on a global survey, regional reserves, and reserves within individual producer nations.

Since the close of the World Food Conference in 1974, FAO has coordinated the efforts to reach agreement on the International Undertaking on World Food Security, which plans for these national and regional reserves. However, the entire process has gone poorly, thanks especially to the uncooperative attitude of the United States. A number of nations have agreed to the plan and are preparing targets, reserve policies and storage facilities. Yet today, India is the only nation that has established significant reserve holdings, largely on its own initiative. After drawing on these reserves for two years, India has now paid $300 million in cash to purchase 1.5 million metric tons of wheat from the United States to replenish them.[42]

(b) The World Food Council

The World Food Council, established by the World Food Conference in 1974, coordinates the work of all agencies within the UN system dealing with food production, nutrition, food security, food trade and aid. The most recent global meeting on world hunger was the meeting of this Council on May 25-27, 1981 in Novi Sad, Yugoslavia. The presence of 32 cabinet ministers from the 36 countries represented on the Council indicates that governments are taking this work seriously.

The Council noted that the IMF exerts pressure on poorest nations to produce more cash crops for export and stated in its report, "Fifteen of the poorest countries in the world devote more acres to cash crops for export than to food for their own hungry people."

The Council has adopted an eight-part "net" to insure enough food in the world to avoid mass starvation at some future time and to work toward enough food for all of earth's people:

1. Creation of a food facility within the IMF. First suggested by FAO and commended in the Brandt Report, the facility has been created and will provide financial assistance to low-income members of the IMF who encounter trouble paying high costs for cereal imports during times of crop failure.

2. A new international wheat agreement. The proposal is to stabilize wheat prices and create reserves through stockpiling. However, the five large transnational grain corporations of the U.S. make much of their profit from price fluctuations. These corporations in large part control the international wheat market, and also help influence the American position, which is to oppose the agreement.

3. A food aid convention. This part of the net became operational in July 1980 when northern grain producing nations began to guarantee a level of food aid for developing countries. The present agreement is for 7.6 million tons per year.

4. The World Food Programme. Established in 1961 as a joint UN-FAO program, it assists pre-school and school feeding projects and operates food-for-work projects through the UN system.

5. Emergency reserves. Governments indicate the amount of cereals or cash they will place at the disposal of the World Food Programme. The reserve stocks have never reached the low target figure of 500,000 tons.

6. National planning. Developing countries need to expand their capacity to increase production and improve distribution of food. Under the program each country is aided in developing a national food strategy.

7. Access to grain. This provision amounts to a pledge from

grain producing countries not to manipulate the market so as to drive up prices during times of shortage, or eliminate the possibility of grain purchases by poor nations when others can pay higher prices.

8. <u>A food crisis contingency reserve.</u> If world production were to drop dramatically and cereal in store were not sufficient to meet pressing needs, this reserve would be released as the "last resort."[43]

(c)   American Farmer-Owned System of Reserves

The United States, while opposing grain reserves under the auspices of FAO, did pass the Farm Act of 1977 which created a farmer-owned reserve system in which American farmers hold some surplus grain. The Act also called for a four-million-ton reserve of wheat to backstop the PL-480 program, so Food for Peace does not have to go into the open market and buy grain in competition during a time of shortage.

The farmer-owned reserve program has been modestly successful in keeping domestic and world grain prices from reaching extreme highs or lows. However, the actual level of stocks is very inadequate to provide protection in the event of serious production setbacks. According to most experts, reasonable world security would require reserves of 60 to 80 million tons of grain. Moreover, the price at which sales are triggered probably needs to be raised an additional 10 to 15 percent over current levels, if the twin objectives of preserving the reserve against premature depletion and protecting farm income are to be achieved. However, the price at which release is made should be ·kept flexible to take into account changing circumstances.

While this American grain reserve program is useful and could be an integral part of a global strategy, it is insufficient by itself and should be seen only as a way-station to implementation of the plans adopted by FAO following the World Food Conference of 1974.

(d)   UN High Commissioner for Refugees

The UN High Commissioner for Refugees has been busy working out agreements for temporary assistance in countries around the world where there are refugees. Much of the work is in the form of direct assistance, but perhaps an even more significant role is that of officially coordinating the efforts of a host of government and private organizations when they enter to work with newly-created refugee programs. UNHCR provides legal protection for refugees and gives them humanitarian, non-political aid in starting new lives. This can be done better by an official global organization which is not bound to any particular national interest.

(e)   UNDP: Its Special Role

The United Nations Development Program (UNPD) has its own aid program which is similar to that conducted by many governments. In many instances, the UN is welcomed where the United States may not be trusted. Increasingly, UNDP is the organization that works closely with the planning departments of governments to design total plans of action for a period of years. Then individual nations and development organizations step forth to accept particular parts of the total plan as their share. United States continued support for UNDP is a vital part of this nation's commitment to third world development.

(f) Other UN Programs

Other important UN programs which are targeted at specific needs and which deserve strong support are only briefly mentioned here. They include:

* UN International Children's Emergency Fund (UNICEF) which helps children through community based services in health, nutrition, social welfare and education;

* International Development Association (IDA) which assists the least developed countries by making loans on easier terms than are ordinarily available;

* International Finance Corporation (IFC) which encourages private enterprise, particularly in less developed countries, providing managerial and technical support for selected projects;

* International Fund for Agricultural Development (IFAD) which helps to finance food production through grants for studies, training and research; and

* UN Industrial Development Organization (UNIDO) which helps less developed countries establish new industries or improve existing ones.

The UN, through UNDP, its participating agencies and special funds, provides technical assistance in specific projects. The development banks are the main channels of capital. The Brandt Report suggests that agencies have proliferated both inside and outside the UN system so that now "their policies, programs and procedures need to be more effectively coordinated and concerted." The report continues, "There is need to monitor the entire assistance system, to reduce the dispersion of effort, to identify shortfalls, to promote initiatives, to fill gaps and to make aid-giving organizations more accountable and comprehensible...."[44]

U.S. Direct Aid Programs

(a) Presidential Commission Recommendations

The Presidential Commission on World Hunger appointed by President Carter felt that American aid could best be expressed on three broad fronts:

> * by easing the technical burdens and institutional barriers to building self-reliant food systems in developing nations;

* by increasing the earnings opportunities of poor nations and poor individuals; and

* in the short run, by providing food and financial resources in ways that will serve, directly and indirectly, to increase food consumption and improve nutritional levels among the very poor.

The specific findings that came from this Commission are generally intelligent and can provide the basis for public policy changes that will help the cause of eliminating world hunger. Some of these findings bear listing at this point:

1. The U.S. Development Assistance effort continues to be shaped by a narrow concept of national security that frequently conflicts with long range development goals.

2. Shamefully low appropriations for official development assistance prevent the program from attaining its own -- and Congress' -- stated objectives.

3. In addition to budgetary constraints, U.S. domestic political considerations and special interests dilute the impact of development assistance programs on third world societies.

4. The short-term authorization and one-year appropriation currently used for foreign assistance impede rational planning and consistent implementation of programs -- for donors and recipients alike.

5. There is a widepread perception that the NEW DIRECTIONS aid guidelines preclude support for institution building and physical infrastructure projects, and that capital development is inconsistent with a "Basic Human Needs" development strategy. While constant attention is required to ensure that such projects do not increase disparities in economic and political power, foreign assistance programs do need flexibility to permit support for some activities which increase income and provide the foundation for long-term and equitable development, even though in the short run they may not benefit the poor directly.

6. During the past decade there has been a significant decline in the capacity of AID to provide high quality technical assistance to help recipient nations sustain self-reliant national agricultural systems.

7. U.S. institutions of research and higher learning do not now make their maximum contribution to the war on hunger.

8. Land tenure policies in many developing countries severely retard food and agricultural production and distribution. Therefore, U.S. policy should support agrarian reforms that produce more equity in land tenure patterns.

9. Many AID programs are meeting vital needs that otherwise would not be met for at least a generation. For example, in Bangladesh, the wheat crop has increased 600 percent in four years. The U.S., via AID, the World Bank and other programs, has contributed greatly to this result.

10. The U.S. Food Aid Program should be used far more purposefully than at present to ensure that malnourished people in poor countries derive the maximum benefits and suffer no unintended harm.[45]

(b) Does AID Hurt or Help the Poor?

Jack Nelson, in his book Hunger for Justice,[46] takes the position that U.S. aid to developing countries is a form of neo-colonialism in that it creates a continuing dependence on outside resources. Further, he feels that "aid, in its variety of forms, is an instrument of American foreign policy. Its purpose is not and never has been to help the poor and hungry."

Nelson sees aid as a device for securing access to foreign markets and raw materials, with uniformly adverse affects on the poor of recipient countries. To him, PL-480 has been a "Food for War" program (Viet Nam) and has undercut poor nation food producers. Among other evils, it fosters poor country indebtedness and dependence.[47]

How do we answer Nelson and others who feel that aid is evil and should be stopped? We begin by acknowledging a significant element of truth in his analysis, but also state our view that his presentation is one-sided. He does not tell the success stories, nor does he point to the reforms that have occurred within AID.

Nelson makes a case against poor country participation in the international economic system by pointing out that in 1900 the South had a per capita income about half that of the rich nations, but by 1970 it was only one-fortieth in 1970 dollars. One can question whether these nations and peoples would have fared better had they chosen a course of economic isolation. One can ask, in this age of interdependence, whether it is a reasonable course to seal one's borders and go it alone. It is hard to turn back the clock to a more simple age. The direction of the future is not isolation but participation. The call for justice will necessarily come within that framework.

At the same time, the churches can provide a service to developing nations by reminding them that the U.S. emphasis on extreme materialism is not necessarily the best model in values for them, and that each country needs to find its own mixture of industrialization and traditional values.

Harnessing the Multinational Corporations

(a)   Size and Power of Multinationals

Multinational corporations are among the most influential actors in global economic life today. By the year 2000 several hundred MNCs will probably own between one-half and four-fifths of the world's productive assets.

The sheer economic power of these large corporations tends to overwhelm struggling nations of the South. This is understandable when one realizes that the "annual sales of GM or Exxon easily exceed the gross national products of Venezuela, Argentina, or South Korea; the annual sales of IBM, GE, or Unilever surpass the GNP of Thailand, Egypt, or Pakistan."[48]

(b)   Need for Accountability

A basic problem with the multinational corporation is there has been nobody to whom it is accountable except stockholders who want short-term profits. The United States has had a long and checkered historical involvement with regulating corporations in order to assure the American people that the public interest is served. When these corporations operate on a global scale, they can in many instances outmaneuver administrators of countries in the making of original agreements, continue to exert undue influence in the political arena, and can drain developing countries of financial resources by transferring assets from one country to another or from one corporate entity to another. Moreover, they usually enter into alliances with middle and upper class elites. Often, the result is to promote products and technologies that satisfy the needs for luxuries for the few, but only create frustration in the appetites of the masses.

(c)   Special Concern for Agribusiness Corporations

Finally, many agribusiness corporations purchase large tracts of land, take ownership away from peasant farmers and then employ on a seasonal basis these same people as marginal workers. The land that had been used to grow crops for local consumption is then used for different crops and exported to feed the middle class of northern nations. By having a virtual monopoly over particular markets, these same corporations can control prices and production schedules for their own benefit, often at the expense of the host country.

For these and other reasons, HUNGER concluded that, on balance, the multinational corporation hinders development and should be curbed or controlled whenever possible.[49]

(d)   A Positive View of Multinationals

The other side of the ledger should be examined also. MNCs do have the technical capacity to mine, manufacture, manage, distribute, and sell goods and services on a large scale. In addition to providing employment, they often provide extensive opportunities for education and training of their employees. For example, International Telephone and Telegraph regularly

has more foreign nationals in training than are present in American colleges
and universities from all nations of the world.

In many countries, models are emerging for a more equitable relationship between the MNC and the host government. In nations as diverse as
Venezuela and Nigeria, multinationals are required to hold no more than a
minority position, with most stock being owned and controlled by either the
government or nationals within the country. In African countries such as
Zimbabwe and Angola, development plans have been made apart from the interests of particular MNCs, and then the corporations have been invited to
participate, but with limited power. The Government of Angola, for example,
has recognized the need for Gulf Oil in its country; the large oil giant is
willing to stay in a subservient role because it is profitable to do so and
because a steady supply of oil is thus assured for Gulf -- even when a majority interest is owned by the state.

This writer takes the position that it does little good to wish that
these corporations would fold their tents and slip away into the night. They
are here to stay and their influence will grow because they provide services
that are perceived to be needed. However, there is urgent need to provide
international controls over these giants, to assist developing nations to
bargain intelligently and to provide assistance necessary to assure mutual
benefits to both hosts and guest corporations.

(e) UN Commission on Transnational Corporations

The most important way to approach this problem for the long term is
for the United States to support the UN Commission on Transnational Corporations (UNCTC). This organization is working towards the development of a
comprehensive Code of Conduct for MNCs which contains provisions dealing
with bribery, transfer pricing, tax policies and disclosure of vital information. UNCTC also provides nations of the South with the technical capacity to
analyze corporate offers and with model agreements that help the nations get
better terms from the corporations.

Other UN agencies are also working on global standards and controls
for MNCs. UNCTAD has completed work on a voluntary international code on
restrictive business practices and is working on a code to govern the transfer
of technology. The International Labor Organization (ILO) is developing a
code for fair labor standards, and the World Health Organization (WHO) has
now written and had adopted a code governing the promotion and marketing of
infant formula and other commercial baby foods. While the United States
opposed the recent international decision to set standards of conduct for
MNCs in the sale of commercial baby foods, these standards were, in fact, set
and the resulting publicity made millions of Americans aware of the problem
in new and positive ways.

Likewise, American citizens can help to control those corporations
which are based in this country through legislation and regulations designed
to curb excesses abroad and make them more sensitive to the real needs and

rights of the developing nations.

(f) Legislation to Curb Multinationals

Hunger lists legislative proposals which in the judgment of the sponsors will be beneficial for poor nations. Suggestions which have appeal to the writer and are still timely are:

* Anti-dumping legislation (HR 6587), sponsored by Representative Michael Barnes of Montgomery County, Maryland, which would "restrict the export of goods which have been found to be hazardous to the public health."

* Grain export sales reporting legislation (HR 4992), sponsored by Representative Neal Smith (D-Iowa) which would provide for timely disclosure of sales of grain for export by U.S. grain companies and their subsidiaries. (Grain merchants may have a more powerful cartel than oil, and their power structures are shrouded in greater secrecy.)

* Legislation should be revised which requires the U.S. Treasury to support U.S.-based MNCs in the event of an investment dispute. In effect, corporations can place business interests above human needs and other foreign policy considerations, and the U.S. government must support them. This program is tied to the Overseas Private Investment Corporation which insures U.S.-based MNCs against war, expropriation, or inconvertability of currency.

In summary, multinationals need much stricter control and accountability than has been exercised over them in the past. Nations are moving in the direction of harnessing these great engines for technical progress. A great deal more can and must be done through United Nations agencies and through the American legislative process to insure that their expertise is used but that the public interest is also served, especially in meeting the needs of the poor in developing nations.

Arms Reduction and World Hunger

No discussion on world hunger in today's world can fail to call attention to the global proliferation of armaments and the expanding U.S. Defense Department budget.

On August 7, 1981 David Stockman met with Secretary of Defense Caspar Weinberger and argued that real defense spending in 1981 is 19 percent above last year, and is 9.4 percent above the Carter projection for increased spending. Stockman was arguing for a slow-down in armament spending in light of the new predicted $70 billion budget deficit for 1981.[50]

Another article on the op-ed page of the Washington Post the same day presented a West German analysis on U.S. military policy:

> The allies have watched with fascination the
> seven-month tug-of-war between Reagan's
> conservative ideologues ("The Weinbergers")
> and the conservative pragmatists ("The Haigs").

> They note that all the administration has come
> up with so far is the simplistic notion to
> arm, arm, arm. An elusive superiority seems
> to be the goal. There is no concept of arms
> control or arms limitation.[51]

The trend toward expansion of military force is continuing world-wide at an accelerated pace -- it apes the actions of the superpowers and is stimulated by them. Consider these facts:

* Military expenditures have now gone beyond $500 billion a year.
* The US-USSR arms race accounts for 58 percent of the total.
* Half of the scientists and engineers in the U.S. direct their knowledge to military purposes.
* The training of military personnel in the U.S. alone costs twice as much per year as the education budget for the 300,000,000 school-age children in South Asia.
* With a stockpile of nuclear weapons, 1,000,000 times the destructive power of the Hiroshima bomb, the two superpowers still invest over $100 million daily to upgrade their nuclear arsenals.
* The world arms trade in 1978 was $21 billion, with over two-thirds of it going to developing nations.[52]

There is a close correlation between wilting economic conditions and the flourishing military sector worldwide. Funds are diverted from meeting human needs, as are materials and trained personnel. Inflation in the world economy has caused consumer prices to double on an average since 1973 when the first oil price jump occurred. We attribute much of the inflation to renewable energy prices; however, inflation is also a close partner of militarization. Military spending overheats the civilian economy by generating more spendable income than goods and services to absorb it.

The task of the churches seems clear in these circumstances. As Alan Geyer stated succinctly:

> Engaging in the struggle to end the nuclear arms
> race is the clearest command of prophetic faith in
> our generation. Most likely, conventional and
> nuclear proliferation are mutually reenforcing
> processes. Both must be reversed. Understanding
> the risks of the conventional arms race in escala-
> ting the possibilities of nuclear war must be a
> constant theme in Christian worship, study and
> action.... It is, even more, a requirement of
> justice to the world's poorest and hungriest
> peoples, to whom the promise of bombers beaten
> into plowshares and missiles into pruning hooks
> has massive poignancy.[53]

CHAPTER TWO

THE CHURCHES AND WORLD HUNGER SINCE 1974

> The earth has enough for every man's need but not for
> every man's greed.
>
> Mahatma Gandhi

The churches have always understood the words of Jesus, "I was hungry
and you gave me food...thirsty and you gave me drink...."

American people, led by their churches, respond with generosity to
appeals for those who are victims of war, drought, flood or other natural
disaster. The United States contributed $81 million or 18% of the U.N. regu-
lar budget in 1980, $70 million or 15.6% of the assessment for specialized a-
gencies, $34 million or 59% for peacekeeping, but $265 million or 59% of the
total for voluntary and special humanitarian programs.[1]

Americans live with the mythology that anyone with common sense and
basic good health can earn a living if she or he is willing to work. Americans
are irritated and even angered by the thought of development assistance going
to the able in routine circumstances and they have no conception of the
structural causes of world poverty and hunger. But they understand how a
flood, hurricane or drought can cause damage for which the individual is not
responsible. Such bad fortune of an emergency nature deserves a helping
hand. Likewise, victims of war elicit sympathy and succor. They are the
innocent who have been driven from their homes, cut off from normal means of
livelihood.

This basic mind-set of Americans was formed in the crucible of the
frontier where anyone willing to work could stake out a farm and make a living
from it. Neither educational institutions nor churches have taught Americans
that the circumstances today in an interdependent global society are different. Therefore, it has been hard to sustain support for development and
even more difficult to acquire a mindset which wants to change the structures
of the international economic order.

When the U.S. foreign aid program began with Harry Truman's Point IV
Program, it followed the Marshall Plan for the economic recovery of Europe.
Many Americans saw this new aid as a temporary expedient like the Marshall
Plan and assumed that if we gave generously the problems would be solved
quickly and we could withdraw. Also, most aid was sold on the basis of using

it as a tool in a worldwide struggle against Soviet communism. When countries that received aid moved back and forth between the Soviet and American sides, depending on where they could get the best deal, we were dismayed.

In the 1980s, there is for many a sense of revulsion toward our "giveaway" programs. The average person tends to feel that with all the help we have given as generous Americans, third world people must be lazy, stupid or corrupt -- perhaps all three -- since they are still in poverty and are still hungry. A growing self-centeredness and "me first" attitude leaves many others not wanting to compromise their own standard of living to sacrifice for hordes of faceless people in far away countries who are not willing to help themselves.

Dispelling this lingering mythology is a prerequisite to action on getting at the real causes of global poverty and hunger.

In order to set the stage for the current response of the churches to systemic causes underlying world hunger, let us go back to 1974, a critical year of world food crisis, and a year in which the churches came alive with the desire to respond.

I.   THE WORLD FOOD CONFERENCE: AMERICA'S MANY VOICES

The World Food Conference of 1974 was held at a time when world food reserves were critically low. Had crops been bad the following year, millions of people might have starved. American churches became aroused by the food issue as the impending crisis emerged and exerted a strong pressure on the United States government to take a humanitarian posture on public food policy. They also began massive programs of relief and rehabilitation which continue in modified form today. But before viewing the role of the churches, let us look at the many official voices within the American government as they responded to this world food crisis. (The writer was close enough to some of the actors to get an inside view which is described below.)

The Political Dilemma

Let us look over the shoulder of President Gerald Ford as he struggled with possible responses to the level at which the U.S. would provide food aid during the closing days of 1974 and the first months of 1975. As the new President prepared to light the nation's Christmas tree, he contended with conflicting advice from his staff and from Congress.

The American delegation had just returned from the historic first World Food Conference in Rome. Secretary of Agriculture Earl Butz, who headed the American delegation, represented agribusiness. His policy was to sell food on the open market to the highest bidder among the nations, as he had recently done with the Soviet Union. Any surplus the U.S. chose to stockpile, he declared, should be stored in America and kept under its control. Henry Kissinger, Secretary of State, had flown to Rome to give the keynote address. Indeed, it was he who first proposed the Conference in a speech at the United Nations in September. The American delegation did not know what he would say; it was typical of Dr. Kissinger in power struggles to keep his cards close to his chest. His public utterances were more humane than those of Mr. Butz; he saw food problems in the context of global interdependence. Privately, and in subsequent input to Mr. Ford, he viewed food as a powerful tool of diplomacy to be used in much the same way the Arabs used oil, for America's economic and political benefit.

The American delegation at the Conference included Senator Clark of Iowa, Senator Hatfield of Oregon, Senator Humphrey of Minnesota, Senator McGovern of South Dakota, and Congressman duPont of Delaware. These men got appointed because they were concerned. They all advocated a strong humanitarian stance on the use of American food during the world hunger emergency. They were outspoken against the policy of Mr. Butz. They represented and indeed were greatly influenced by church leaders of almost every major denomination who attended the meetings in Rome as unofficial observers. Spokespersons for the churches wanted to feed the starving at once and then use American technology, farmlands, and financial resources to develop a long-range program to increase food supplies so that every person on earth could have a sufficient diet. The vision of a world without hunger was becoming more focused.

Dr. Kissinger had flown to Rome, spoken, and left. Mr. Butz had hedged and refused to commit the country. The Congressional delegation had openly petitioned President Ford to announce a generous increase in American food aid for the immediate future, while they publicly denounced what they felt was the miserliness of the Agriculture Secretary.

Mr. Ford delayed. The Conference ended without an indication of American commitment. Before going on a skiing trip to Vail, Colorado, the President promised to announce the level and kind of food aid he would propose for 1975. The bickering among his advisors became intense. Mr. William Simon of the Treasury Department reminded the new President of the need for foreign currency from the sale of grain to balance the heavy outflow of dollars for oil. Mr. Alan Greenspan, Chairman of the Council of Economic Advisors, reminded him that this decision would affect the critical fight against inflation. With short supplies, he intoned, if we give away large quantities of food, we increase the scarcity and hence drive up prices for housewives at the supermarket.

Previously, the United States had committed a billion dollars for food aid, about the same dollar figure as for 1974. But with the increased costs of wheat, corn, soybeans and rice, the hungry of the world would receive almost one-third less for the same billion dollars. The Congressmen who had been at Rome urged that, as a minimum, we give as much in actual quantity as during the previous year, especially in light of the severe droughts and crop shortages in the Sahel of Africa, in India, Bangladesh and some other sections of Southeast Asia. Ten million people, they felt, might die during the year unless food was available.

The State Department entered the debate again to make a strong case for using surplus food for political ends. Dr. Kissinger and his staff argued that food was a commodity like oil, copper, or any other good. Indeed, under his tutelage the administration had already decided tentatively to portion the billion dollars of food aid in such fashion that the great majority would go to Vietnam and Cambodia, since Congress had restricted the President in the amount of additional arms that he could send, and since food aid was left to the discretion of the Executive Branch. Why not, they asked, increase the food supply there, thus releasing purchasing power to buy guns and other war materials? Next, the policy makers of the State Department saw an opportunity to gain both the good will and economic dependence of Egypt and Syria by supplying them with food, with the hope of moving these two volatile countries toward a more restrained position in the Middle East.

But that was not all. Privately, Dr. Kissinger presented a plan to the President whereby the U.S. could break an agreement it had made with South Korea in which it was to receive substantial quantities of imported textiles and shoes. American unions were putting pressure on the government to back away from that commitment, arguing accurately that U.S. workers faced cutbacks and layoffs. A political deal seemed possible; the United States would give larger quantities of food to Korea, and in turn, Korea would agree to break the agreement on imports to this country. At the same time, Indonesia, a fortunate beneficiary of off-shore oil strikes, was willing for American companies to explore and develop oil fields with favored-nation status if the United States would provide additional free food for her rapidly expanding population. With the U.S. need to be free from Arab oil captivity, this was also an enticing prospect.

Weighing this conflicting advice was more than President Ford could handle without consulting his staff. He therefore asked the Office of Management and Budget to present him with options from which he would choose. The Washington Star-News leaked the story about the options which were to be presented. Option one was to limit food to the billion dollar amount and distribute it according to the formula of the previous year. Option two was to increase the total significantly and divide it between food for humanitarian uses and political purposes. Options three and four were to increase the total with the extra amount going in one instance for political uses and in the other for humanitarian ends.

The Christmas tree was lighted. The President went to Vail. But there was no announcement. The Ambassador of Bangladesh waited to see how many of his countrymen would live or starve during January. Many American church leaders "watched and prayed."

While President Ford delayed, the Congress, led by Senator Mark Hatfield, passed legislation making it mandatory that no more than 30 percent of the food in our "Food for Peace" program could be used for political purposes. The remainder must be distributed, they decreed, according to poverty needs among the forty poorest countries of the world as determined by the United Nations.

That legislation created a problem for Dr. Kissinger who was finding additional uses to which food could be put in diplomacy. On February 1, 1975 there was still no announcement of the proposed level of food aid. Then it came. It was almost hidden in the new budget, released on February 2 in a line item for food. It was $1.6 billion, a significant increase. Speculation in the Senate dining room was that the surprisingly large sum was accepted at Dr. Kissinger's insistence because he needed a significant amount for political purposes, albeit only 30 percent of the total.

A New Awakening Within the Churches

The churches, working especially with Senators Hatfield and Humphrey, felt a strong sense of victory and accomplishment for their role in passing the legislation which directed food to the poorest, and for arousing public opinion in favor of a larger total amount. Nonetheless, they knew that victory was relative and temporary. With the prospect of possible massive famine ahead, almost every denomination began to prepare resolutions on world hunger for vote at official conventions or assemblies. Denominational executives began to plan for massive fund-raising campaigns within the parishes to support the feeding of the hungry. Most of them also prepared statements on public policy with the recognition that government policy far outweighed direct action of the churches in terms of the total impact that could be made on world hunger. In short, the world food crisis, coupled with the World Food Conference in Rome, galvanized the churches into action and created a kind of awareness that had not existed since the period of reconstruction following World War II.

This review of a brief moment in history in the nation's response to the perceived food crisis is instructive in several ways: (1) It reveals the power of agribusiness interests to influence policy makers to the end that they make the maximum profit from food regardless of humane interests, as represented in Mr. Butz; (2) it points up the conflict between those who see food as another commodity with which to bargain for perceived American interests, and those who consider it to be in a different category in its life-sustaining capacity; (3) it shows the value of global conferences in dealing with global problems. The reality of interdependence struck home for millions of people who never before considered it seriously. And finally, (4) it reveals the strength of the religious and humanitarian community within the United States when they can agree on a clearcut issue in the midst of a crisis.

II. THE CHURCHES' RESPONSE TO PL-480 PROGRAMS

American churches have conducted food distribution programs since World War II and at many other times previously. In the period we are surveying, beginning with 1974, the role of churches and church-related agencies expanded as new legislation revised the PL-480 program to provide a larger role for them in the distribution of food aid abroad.

Title II of Food for Peace is a program for feeding mothers and children and is administered by churches and other private voluntary organizations, with the U.S. government providing most of the food.

Most Protestant denominations participated through Church World Service but many also have been involved directly. Lutherans and Roman Catholics have strong programs of their own.

Effectiveness of the Churches

How effective have the churches been in this role? UNICEF sponsored a review of the program and concluded:

> Neither the true effects nor full
> benefits of food distribution programs
> have yet been adequately measured....
> Their nutritional impact upon the
> neediest groups appears to be low.

The Presidential Commission on World Hunger noted that food and nutrition programs are the subject of continuing controversy. With the focus on mothers and children, the programs are politically acceptable in most countries. Much of the distribution is done through existing organized channels. When food is distributed through schools in lunch programs, there is a marked enhancement of learning ability and increased attendance. Negatively, the churches have found it hard to reach out to the poorest and those in distant villages.

The Presidential Commission advocated more experimental approaches including the targeting of areas and groups within areas, with the greatest emphasis on provision of nutrition for pregnant women.[2]

Questions which can serve as the basis for evaluation include:

* Do the food programs emphasize the imperative
   of breast feeding?

* Do they introduce weaning foods?

* Do they teach proper care for children with diarrhea?

* Do they fortify food in basic products such as
   flour, tea, sugar or salt?

* Do they distribute vitamins to meet specific needs
   such as iron deficiency?

* Are programs shaped to meet specific nutritional
   needs of local areas?

Title III of the Food for Peace program also utilizes the churches and other volunteer organizations and has some imaginative programs for agricultural development and community improvement which pay workers in American food. For example, workers build irrigation systems or farm-to-market roads and receive at least part of their pay in food. In this way, they are earning what they receive, at times are learning a skill, and are thus enhancing their future livelihoods.

Inherent Dangers in AID Food Programs

The Food Aid Program has created some problems as well as served a noble and humanitarian purpose. The inherent contradiction in any aid or welfare program is the danger of increasing dependency of the recipients on the donors. At times the churches have found themselves participating in programs where negative consequences were recognized. For example, relief efforts have, on occasion, hurt local farmers by destroying their markets. When large quantities of relief supplies have been given without careful regard to the local economy, the lasting impact has been negative. Some of the potential problems are:

* Danger of depressing the local markets by the influx of significant amounts of food from outside.

* Danger of supporting an inequitable economic system. Unfair treatment of tenants by landlords may be allowed to continue as long as these poor are being fed anyway.

* Danger of stabilizing a repressive government. An inhumane government may use the Food for Peace program to serve as the opiate of the masses and thus continue in power.

* Danger of developing a dependency so that if help is stopped the recipients are in a worse position to help themselves than before.

* Danger of inefficient management and corruption. While the corruption may not involve church staff persons, their indigenous counterparts have at times been able to manipulate the program to sell grain and use the money to their personal advantage. Through association with the American government and church-related personnel there appears to be an implicit failure on the part of the churches.

* Danger of not reaching the truly needy because of inadequate channels of communication with them.

The churches of the nation have struggled to find their proper role in a government-sponsored program in which the purposes of aid are not always humanitarian. By law there are four basic goals of the program:

* Provide humanitarian assistance.

* Spur economic development within recipient nations.

* Develop markets for U.S. agricultural commodities.

* Promote U.S. foreign policy objectives.

The latter goals at times are felt by some church leaders to be in conflict with the former. Food may be sent, not where it is needed the most, but where it can be used to enhance American foreign policy objectives. Because of this deeply felt contradiction and because at times negative consequences were recognized, the religious community has been struggling to decide whether in good conscience it can continue to work in the program. It is asking whether to remain inside and try to improve conditions or to withdraw.

Whether working within as contractors or from the outside as concerned citizens, the churches should continue to seek to influence policies related to the PL-480 Food for Peace program. They should encourage Food for Work programs that subsidize food production while giving food for consumption. As long as people are hungry and malnourished, the Food for Peace program has an important role. It must constantly strive to reach the poorest in the population and be careful not to undermine the efforts of recipient nations to develop a more self-reliant agricultural base of their own.

Food for "Peace" is a questionable title for this program. It implies the need for political motivation, albeit a good one. "Food for People" is sufficient; the churches should constantly teach from the perspective of seeing human beings as ends in themselves, worthy of help without strings attached, because they are human. Yet Christians need to be "wise as serpents while being harmless as doves," always careful to avoid negative consequences of well-intended action.

III. LIBERATION THEOLOGY AND THE GROUP OF 77

The modern missionary movement began when European explorers discovered the world. These Europeans, and much later the Americans, took the church to what we now call the third world by sending thousands of missionaries. These Christian workers felt called to share the good news of Jesus Christ through evangelism, building churches, and starting schools, hospitals and other social institutions.

As the colonial powers released their domination over the colonies, their counterparts in the mission program became aware that they as foreigners were also dominating the churches and related social institutions. A self-conscious change began to occur in most denominations -- a real effort was made to share control of the churches with indiginous Christians. It was not easy to change the image or the pattern. Even when Northern churches became aware, they hesitated to give money without controls. Inevitably, mission is still defined as "something Northern churches do."

The World Council of Churches Commission on World Mission and Evangelism, at its Bangkok Conference in 1973, stated the dilemma clearly:

> Even when autonomy and equal partnership have
> been achieved in a formal sense, the actual
> dynamics are such as to perpetuate relationships
> of domination and dependence.

American church leaders are painfully aware, too, that when control is passed, the enthusiasm for giving and supporting missionaries is dampened. The United Presbyterian Church USA was in the forefront of acting on the new requirement of breaking dependency. At the time the denomination was formed in 1958, it supported 1,300 missionaries. These church-supported workers abroad are now called "fraternal workers" -- but the number has dropped to 400. Meanwhile, Southern Baptists have hardly bothered to raise the question of domination or dependency, and they have steadily increased the number of missionaries since 1958 from some 1,200 to 2,500.

Liberation Theology: Empowering the Poor

Many of the churches in the third world have embraced a "liberation theology." What poor peoples and nations require, they feel, is for them to gain control of their own economic destiny and become liberated from the dominance of foreign economic power, as well as from the landlords and other wealthy elites in their own countries. For some, this liberation means a break with all types of development assistance. This new understanding is gained by a new reading of the Bible as a liberation document.

Gutierrez objected to the papal encyclical of 1967, far-reaching though it was. It was addressed to the "great ones of this world urging them to carry out the necessary changes." Gutierrez suggested that it should have been addressed to the oppressed to encourage them to "break with their present situation and take control of their own destiny."[3]

Conventional wisdom in the field of development says that if you give a man a fish he will eat for a day, but teach him how to fish and he can eat for the rest of his life. But that will not happen, suggests Tracy Early, if other people have a monopoly on use of the fishing stream. Liberation theology urges the hungry person to gain access to a fishing place. If he can get access, he will probably teach himself how to catch the fish. Freedom of access is the key to a full stomach.

That is why the delegates at World Council of Churches at Nairobi arrived at a definition of development that defined the process as "a liberating process aimed at justice, self-reliance and economic growth."[4]

Liberation: The Goal of the Group of 77

The unwanted cloak of political domination can finally be shed when third world countries take their destinies into their own hands. They are trying to organize among themselves in order to gain the opportunity for a more equitable share of wealth in the international economy. This is precisely the goal of the Group of 77. Yet the response of the churches of the United States has been muted or nonexistent in support of this effort. Rather than rally behind this legitimate claim for justice by the nations where we have sent our missionaries, the American churches have either not understood what is at stake, or they have largely ignored it. A case can be made for the statement that western church domination will not end until economic and political neo-colonialism have given way to the new international economic order.

IV. RECENT CHURCH-SPONSORED DEVELOPMENT PROJECTS

In response to the world hunger crisis in 1974, western churches began new hunger programs and expanded old ones. Then rather quickly the crisis faded. Nonetheless, the churches had caught a glimpse of the debilitating nature of world hunger and were determined to follow through on the momentum that had been generated. They reasoned that the deeper need of the poor is aid that will enable people to feed themselves and develop their own economies. So the emphasis has shifted to small-scale economic development in the context of enhancing human potential. Most denominations now sponsor significant small-scale development projects.

Some within the churches are asking now if there is a Biblical mandate to work in the field of development. Certainly, there is no chapter and verse to cite for programs of economic development. But Christian concern for the welfare of people for whom Christ died may lead to programs of development sponsored by the churches. On the other hand, as Tracy Early points out, churches want to be "relevant" and development may seem to be the "in" thing to do. Mr. Early questioned whether Christ's command to "feed my sheep" means that the church should operate restaurant franchises.[5]

The World Council of Churches since 1970 has had a Commission on the Churches' Participation in Development. It has emphasized the development of people as well as material resources. This writer believes that it is a positive step for the churches to become involved in development projects. The involvement gives the churches and those individuals who work in the projects a sense of participation, and provides an opportunity for empathy with suffering people and an awareness of the difficulties of changing entrenched social structures. But, at best, these are only "signs" or pilot projects in comparison to the totality of the task ahead, and they must never be substituted for the more important task of eliminating hunger throughout the world by challenging the structures of institutions.

V. RECENT RESPONSES TO CRISES OF WORLD HUNGER

To make a general assessment of the role the churches have played in emergency relief and rehabilitation in recent years, let us look very briefly at the two most recent crises in Cambodia and Somalia.

Cambodian Relief and Rehabilitation

> In the hospital we visited in Kampong Speu there were 485 patients, 200 beds, 13 nurses and no doctors. A shelter full of children with worried eyes and thin bodies, too weak to cry, sat watching us as we stood silently trying to absorb the sights, sounds, and smells of that awful place. They were the

> fortunate ones. They at least were getting
> some food. Others are still in the country-
> side. The civilians under the control of
> the Pol Pot forces in Western Kampuchea
> are in much worse shape, according to
> all reports.[6]

By March of 1979 it was evident to those willing to look that a substantial relief effort would have to be mounted in Cambodia. The task would be difficult because the Pol Pot government opposed the presence of westerners in their country and because starvation of the masses was a deliberate strategy for winning the war. It took the world community six months to make a significant beginning on this relief effort. By mid-October 1979, however, a joint program was launched by the United Nations Children's Fund (UNICEF) and the International Committee of the Red Cross (ICRC), funded by governments and private contributions. Very soon the private voluntary agencies, including the churches, began their own large scale efforts in a cooperative way, working under the general direction of the two major bodies that coordinated the total effort. These included the American Friends Service Committee, Catholic Relief Services, Church World Service, World Council of Churches, Oxfam, World Vision International and many others.

On October 19, 1979 UNICEF and ICRC launched a formal appeal for government funds which eventually amounted to a request for $251 million. At a U.N. pledging conference on November 5, $210 million was pledged by representatives of 57 nations. On October 24, a group of 40 religious and humanitarian leaders had appealed to President Carter and UN Secretary General Kurt Waldheim for action, and then issued appeals directly to churches and others in the private sector for individual contributions. President Carter announced a $69 million U.S. contribution to the international aid fund. Of this amount Congress quickly appropriated $30 million of new money.

Somalian Relief and Rehabilitation

The Somalian crisis was a long time in the making but has gotten world attention only recently. The Somalians are by tradition a proud and self-sufficient people who were loathe to ask for help.

Most Somalians are nomads who depend upon their goats, camels and sheep for sustenance. At age five each child is given a goat to own and tend. The elders become teachers, and children learn hundreds of grasses, herbs and shrubs that can provide medicinal benefit for animals and people.

Most of the refugees have come from the Ogoden, a region inhabited by the ethnic Somalians, but not a part of that nation. The region reaches to the Indian Ocean. Ethiopia has long aspired to extend its boundaries across this area. As a result, Ethiopia and Somalia have been fighting intermittently for ten years over the region.

Prior to 1977 the Soviets supplied arms to Somalia, but with the growing opportunity for influence in Ethiopia, the USSR asked Ethiopia and Somalia to join hands in a united Soviet-based region. When Somalia refused to join her old enemy, Soviet support shifted: $2 billion in military supplies and equipment was sent over a few months to Ethiopia.

The United States, alarmed by the apparent potential control of the region by the USSR, began to supply arms to Somalia, thus making a region where hostilities had been deep but the ability to inflict harm relatively modest, into one of enormous destructive capacity. Now herds can be wiped out in minutes, and life-giving wells of water can be poisoned at will.

Food is gone and life is dangerous for the people in the Ogoden, so many are making the long trek to where their brothers and sisters live in Somalia, and others are going to the Sudan and Kenya. Of the 1.3 million refugees, 1.1 million are Ogoden people.

Compounding the tragedy of the war is a drought which is now in its fifth year. From Ojebouti south through Ethiopia, Somalia, Kenya, Uganda and southern Sudan, "carcasses of cattle and camels are strewn over the parched desert. Farms and grazing lands have been abandoned."

The refugees are 90 percent women and children. They arrive hungry and often seriously ill. Life in the camps is harsh. Malnutrition is widespread and severe. Water is scarce and polluted; medical supplies are often non-existent, and only a few have blankets, despite night temperatures dropping into the 40s. The inhabitants of the 32 refugee camps are now totally dependent on outside food aid supplied by an international relief effort. The daily ration for each refugee as set by the UN World Food Program is 600 grams of food a day. In fact, because of inadequate supplies, the actual amount was until recently only 300 grams, which is barely enough for most people to stay alive.[6]

On April 9-10, 1981, the United Nations held a conference in Geneva to get pledges of support from the nations of the world for the crisis in Africa. Eighty-five nations attended. The goal of the conference was a pledge of $1.3 billion spread over five years to provide emergency aid, and then to help in relocation and rehabilitation of these refugees.

Of the $470 million western package, the United States pledged $285 million and announced that it would accept up to 8,300 refugees over two years "if they want to come."

Ambassador Jean Kirkpatrick, who led the American delegation, announced that $126.5 million of new aid money will go to two organizations -- the UN High Commissioner for Refugees and the International Red Cross -- $80.7 million will go for food aid, $65 million for resettlement of refugees in their countries of origin, and $11.2 million to help those who decide to relocate in the United States.

Ambassador Kirkpatrick explained that the Administration is recommending an increase in aid next year to Africa of 30 percent, but that most of it will go to Somalia and Kenya, which have agreed to give the United States access to military facilities as part of the American buildup in the Indian Ocean.

A strategy for rehabilitation and self-reliance is already being designed by the Somalian government and the United Nations. The United States government, along with private and church-related groups, is being invited to participate in mutually agreeable ways. The plan states:

> An integrated comprehensive strategy for developing
> the entire country must be implemented. New schools,
> hospitals and highways must be built. Land that
> has turned into desert as a result of overgrazing
> must be revitalized and reforested. New agricultural
> areas must be created, fishing expanded, and
> natural resources developed.

Unless a vigorous plan of this kind is implemented, the entire region may become a permanent welfare area, a sea of human misery.

Response of the Churches

What has been the response of the churches in the Somalian relief and rehabilitation program? The pattern followed that for Cambodia: (1) growing awareness and exploration of the problem; (2) urging the American government and United Nations agencies to take action; (3) following the leadership of the United Nations and the International Red Cross; (4) collecting of funds from constituents; (5) direct relief and rehabilitation work in cooperation with those who made a comprehensive plan; (6) education of church bodies and planning for longer-term rehabilitation work; (7) expectation that some work will be done with their own funds and some under contract from government agencies.

This general response seems appropriate to the circumstance. The churches recognize the major role belongs to governments, as they alone can command the funds required for such enormous undertakings. Helping to lobby for government action and then helping to create public acceptance for official spending are proper roles for the churches. At the same time, it is important for churches to be involved directly; the level of understanding and emotional commitment tends to be correlated with the extent of involvement. Yet our churches, like our government, find it more palatable to give relief assistance than to work for systemic changes in the patterns of economic life.

CHAPTER THREE

A CRITICAL REVIEW OF CHURCH-RELATED HUNGER PROGRAMS

> One hard fact must be stated bluntly: the arms race
> goes on, the momentum of the race never slackens,
> and the danger of holocaust is imminent. Meanwhile,
> millions starve, development stagnates and inter-
> national cooperation is threatened.[1]

At this critical time, the Administration in Washington stands almost
alone among the nations in taking the position that third world countries
should not be given more assistance. In fact, between January and September 1,
1981, the Reagan Administration was isolated on five important votes in the
community of nations. The latest came in August in Nairobi at the Energy
Conference, called to design a plan to help poorest countries exploit gas and
oil resources and develop alternate forms of energy. The Programme of Action
-- to cost $1 billion -- was rejected by the U.S.A. Even a $50 million
compromise was rejected with an OMB statement that private enterprise can do
the job, leaving the United States alone against all the countries of the
world.[2]

In this milieu, the churches require a clear sense of direction as
they confront the Reagan Administration on how to deal with systemic causes
underlying world hunger. Then they need to develop an educational program
that will help to dispel outmoded mythologies about why poor nations are that
way. Finally, the churches need a new vigor and imagination as they cooperate
with others to change the structures of the international political economy.

Never has meeting such a challenge been more imperative. Never has
the political climate been more inauspicious.

Now let us turn to a study of denominations and other organizations
related to the churches to determine how they approach systemic causes underlying world hunger.

I. ROMAN CATHOLIC

The Roman Catholic Church is like a mansion with many rooms. Since it
is not possible within the scope of this study to explore or evaluate all of
them, three very diverse groups have been selected. The first is most significant -- the International Justice and Peace Office of the United States
Catholic Conference. The second is a most creative and influential resource
-- the Center of Concern, and the third is a random sample of a conference
conducted by a religious order which is deeply concerned about the hungry of
the world.

The United States Catholic Conference is the creation of the Catholic bishops and serves as their public policy agency. The function of the staff is to advise the bishops, to formulate policies in areas in which the bishops have an interest, to lobby on capitol hill, and then to help educate the clergy and laity at the request of the bishops.

Each Catholic diocese in the United States is an independent entity; the Catholic Conference has no power to dictate any policy or action in a diocese. However, almost every diocese has a Public Affairs Office with from one to several staff members who advise the bishop on social issues and work under his direction in social action, social welfare and education within that jurisdiction. Many of the dioceses use materials prepared by the Conference, utilize its staff as speakers and workshop leaders and look to this organization for leadership.

The Conference makes policies and develops programs from the top down and from the bottom up. When the bishops meet annually, they divide into committees that oversee the various Commissions and Offices within the Conference. A special concern may emerge among the bishops which leads them to take a policy initiative. The other approach is for policy to develop by recommendation from Bishop Kelly, Executive Director, who brings to the other bishops the proposals of staff members working closely with the issue.

The Office most relevant to this study is that of International Peace and Justice, directed by Reverend J. Bryan Hehir. Working under his direction on the staff of the Interreligious Task Force on the U.S. Food Policy is Dr. Henry Brody, a trained economist and specialist on food policy. When testimony is presented to Congressional Committees these two men often share in the preparation. They seek to blend the technical-factual data and the moral meaning, with Dr. Brody writing the social science material and Reverend Hehir providing the input on the moral section. Often the testimony is actually presented by an eminent bishop.

The Office has a four-sided philosophy on policy issues related to world hunger. First, all policy positions are based on the social teachings of the Church. The guidebook that is used is the Gospel of Peace and Justice, a compilation of official social pronouncements since Pope John, beginning May 15, 1961.[3]

Secondly, the Conference takes the position that the central issue is global social justice -- the structure of the international economic order itself. Problems of justice within countries tend to be addressed locally through the Church in those places. For American churchmen, the question has to be: "What do we do?" If we focus on U.S. policy as it relates to the international economic order, we deal with our own greatest responsibility.

Thirdly, in tandem with this central focus is a pervasive use of the concept of interdependence. The category is useful to the Conference because it has an economic content that serves as the basis for foreign policy and a moral-Biblical side that recognizes all people as children of a loving heavenly Father.

Finally, the Conference focuses on problems of hunger more than on the broader issue of world poverty. It recognizes that the hunger issue cannot be seen apart from poverty, human resource development, and a range of other related problems, yet wants to keep the focus very clearly on hunger. The Conference does not want to "dissolve the problem in such a way as to deny it."[4]

The program to combat world hunger has grown steadily since its inception in 1974. Dr. Walt Grazer of the Conference staff feels the hunger issue has captured the imagination of the Church in the USA more than any other social issue. He feels that it is easier now to raise the hard questions than it was a few years ago because there is now a "hard core constituency" and a wider group with much more sympathy and understanding.

The Conference uses three strategies in its hunger education program. First, it has used the Church in the Third World as teacher. This segment of the Church has made an enormous contribution to the social teachings of the whole body during the past 20 years. Built around liberation, third world theology has brought a new mindset and perspective to the entire Church. Moreover, interaction among missionaries and third world bishops with their counterparts in the United States has helped to create sympathy for political and economic injustices suffered at the hands of the developed world. In El Salvador, for example, the American Church rallied behind Archbishop Romero, and then behind the cause he represented after his murder, with the result that American policy as enunciated by Secretary of State Haig has been modified. Walt Grazer expressed the view that the star of western theology is falling, but that western thinkers are listening to third world experience as they try to rethink what it means to be called by Christ in this era.

Secondly, it has developed an institutional apparatus related to hunger issues at the diocesan level which has grown steadily for the past seven years. Today hunger related issues command more money, staff and literature than previously.

Thirdly, there is a renewed emphasis on Christian living, a higher consciousness of the spiritual side of life. Many bishops hope this will lead to a more sensitive social conscience among the laity, although some of the new groups now espouse inwardness with little concern for the outward journey.

The current hunger emphasis began in 1974 when the National Conference of Catholic Bishops (NCCB) issued "The World Crisis -- A Pastoral Plan of Action." The bishops' action was taken five days after the close of the World Food Conference in Rome. At the Food Conference, Pope Paul had described global hunger as a "crisis of solidarity and civilization." The American bishops felt it was time to mobilize the energies of the Church in response to the needs of the poor and hungry in this country and abroad.

To assist the bishops, the Office of International Peace and Justice published two booklets titled Our Daily Bread; one in January 1975 and a second in September 1975. Volume 2 recognized the extensive degree of involvement the program had elicited throughout the country. The booklet set forth a range of appropriate responses for the Church "at the level of public policy, legislative programs, community information, and education and pastoral practice."

Seven points were presented as the public policy thrust:

* Increase agricultural development overseas.
* Increase funding of Food for Peace.
* Modify U.S. trade policies to lower trade barriers and
    to provide just prices for imports from poor countries.
* Assure American farmers a fair return on capital
    and labor.
* Promote more equitable distribution of resources in the
    United States.
* Promote the family-sized farm.
* Modify the operation of the free market system,
    especially the impact of the large corporations
    when they stand in the way of justice.

In a policy statement, Reverend Bryan Hehir said "...in the energy crisis we are on the receiving end of vulnerability; but in the food crisis we are in the position of power and possession." He then presented the moral perspective when he wrote:

> The perception of social justice focuses
> not upon our motive for giving but upon
> the substance of our policy: aid, trade,
> corporate practices and political purposes.
> Such a structural approach poses our moral
> responsibility not in terms of the option of
> charity but in terms of the duty of justice.

The flavor of the Catholic Conference's recent public policy position on Development can be savored by reviewing testimony before the Senate Foreign Relations Committee on the FY 1982 Foreign Assistance Authorization. Reverend Hehir reviewed the 1982 AID proposals in the light of political, economic and moral interdependence:

> The full meaning of interdependence must be
> seen in moral terms. Interdependence means
> we are locked together in a limited world.
> The decisions we make as states have a direct
> bearing on the welfare and quality of life
> of others.... This recognition of mutual
> vulnerability raises the question of moral
> responsibility.... The category of social
> justice is a central criterion for policy
> when there is only so much for so many.

The testimony called attention to the Brandt Commission Report, the Report of the Presidential Commission on World Hunger, and the Global 2000 Report, all of which presumed interdependence as the basis for policy choices. Yet, he testified, the Reagan Administration has not formulated its policies with proper recognition of interdependence.

> The consensus stands in striking contrast to
> the present direction of U.S. policy as
> expressed in this foreign assistance package.
> The mood of the moment is to deny or at least
> ignore the interdependence of the world as
> a guide for policy.

The USCC then presented its views on specific parts of the proposed Foreign Assistance budget. In summary, USCC:

* decried the real drop in economic development assistance -- the same level of aid has been voted in 1979, 1980 and 1981, with a projected freeze in the funding level until 1985. With inflation, the 1982 budget is 20 percent less than that of three years earlier;

* opposed the 50 percent proposed increase in military assistance and suggested that half of this amount be transferred to economic aid;

* supported the present balance of one-third of all dollars for aid through multilateral institutions and two-thirds for bilateral programs, and opposed efforts to cut back on multilateral support;

* recommended full funding of $3.24 billion for the sixth replenishment of the International Development Association (IDA), to be paid in three equal annual installments;

* urged restoration of the U.S. contribution to the second replenishment of the International Fund for Agricultural Development to the level of $229 million proposed by the Administration; (IFAD efforts are directed to small-scale agricultural projects in the poorest countries;) and

* opposed all military aid for El Salvador but supported increased economic assistance for the poor and victims of war.[5]

Critical Evaluation of USCC

The momentum on hunger-related issues remains strong within the Roman Catholic Church. The Office of International Peace and Justice is strengthened in its prophetic approach to the analysis of systemic issues by the official social teachings of the Church. Many pronouncements since Pope John XXIII have been forthright and prophetic. They provide a sense of security and authority for those who work on these issues.

From the perspective of this paper, the Church in the United States is on the mark when it defines the central issue as the world economic order itself. The emphasis on interdependence as the context for all policy positions is helpful and appropriate.

One can appreciate the desire to keep the focus on hunger and not get so heavily into underlying causes that hunger becomes secondary. This balance is a sensitive one; there is no evidence to the writer that the scales have been tipped too far away from related issues.

The solidarity of the Church as a world institution gives it an advantage; it better hears the cries of oppression from segments of the world where people have been most abused. The surge of vitality that has come from the third world Church provides an enriching stream into the common life, especially for the Church in the United States.

One is impressed by the clarity of the writings and testimony of Reverend Bryan Hehir, Associate Secretary, and Dr. Henry Brody who works directly with the Interreligious Task Force as the Roman Catholic staff person. However, one is also struck with the magnitude of their task when compared with the size of the Church and the roles they are asked to fill. Reverend Hehir gives more than 100 addresses or workshops annually in all parts of the country. This in itself is a full-time job and leaves little time for research, public policy testimony or writing on the emerging issues.

One gets the impression that most of the education is directed to religious orders, making one ask how effective the Office is in reaching to the laity across the Church through the dioceses. Granted that this responsibility rests with each bishop; nonetheless, materials and other resources are needed, along with clear analysis of issues, if laypersons are to come alive in their understanding of systemic issues.

Given the assumption that the international economic order is the central issue, one asks why there is not a stronger involvement with those in the U.S. State Department, Treasury, Department of Agriculture, and the International Trade Commission who make U.S. policies related to the international economic order. It would seem that an active role in the North-South dialogue would be useful as the Group of 77 strives to change the structures of the economic order. One asks at this writing what is being done to influence the Reagan Administration's position on the North-South dialogue, scheduled to take place in Mexico on October 22-23.

In short, this primary instrument of the Church seems understaffed and, therefore, less than well equipped to provide the kind of leadership required on public policy issues and on interpretation and education for this large constituency. The quality of leadership is excellent, but the amount that can be accomplished is limited for so large and important a Church.

Center of Concern

The Center of Concern began in 1971 as an independent organization but also as an arm of the International Jesuit Order. It is composed of an interdisciplinary team of scholars who do policy analysis and serve both policy makers and the 100 Justice and Peace Centers of the Roman Catholic Church throughout the United States.

The Center collaborates with a network of social action/reflection Centers in this country and throughout the world. The Jesuit network has a Center in Paris which serves as headquarters for others. There are ten Centers in Europe, fifteen in Latin America, three in India, and others in every part of the world.

Ecumenical cooperation is a hallmark; currently, the center serves as the Secretariat for the Muslim-Jewish-Christian Conference for Peace and Justice.

There is a staff of three Jesuits, one of whom is Director, Peter J. Henriot, S.J., and four other scholar associates, three of whom are women. The budget for 1980 was $196,506. As an independent Center, funds are raised from three sources: contributions from an annual appeal to a mailing list of 15,000 amounting to $80,000; staff earnings from workshops and publications of $50,000; and grants from foundations, churches and religious organizations of $70,000. The three largest grants in 1980 were from the Society of Jesus, Board of Church and Society of the United Methodists, and the United Auto Workers.

Four areas of concern provide the focus for work: (1) Women in Church and Society, their rights and roles; (2) The Church and Labor, a movement to support trade unions with their important contributions to the future of the global society; (3) Social Theology, a study of Catholic social thought as a guide for the Center's work and as a means of educating others; and (4) Development in the context of the global rich/poor confrontation.

The issue of global hunger is not a separate concern of the Center, but is an important integral part of the Development focus. In the Development effort the Center asks:

> What does a new international economic order
> mean and why is it necessary? What are the
> human effects of trade and investment? What
> forces are at work in the forward self-reliant
> development of the 1980s, and how can they be
> encouraged?[6]

The staff gives a major part of its time to education of religious leaders in Roman Catholic orders. Since its inception in 1971, the Center has conducted more than 3,000 workshops, ranging in length from one day to a week. Most of these are conducted in Justice and Peace Centers. These 100 separate organizations follow no set pattern in their composition. One may be a local sisterhood, another a combination of orders, and a third will have laity participation. They are concerned for a whole range of social justice issues of which world hunger is one.

The Center of Concern is considered by many to take a radical approach to global issues. It does not accept the label, but as an independent organization feels free to constructively criticize all Offices and institutions of Church and society, including the Pope and the American College of

Bishops. The Center does not lobby in the U.S. Congress, although staff members do write letters to the President and members of Congress, and they maintain contact with officers of the State Department, AID, and the staff of the United Nations.

The uniqueness of the Center of Concern, in contrast to all other organizations studied in this paper, is its active involvement in affairs of the United Nations -- in special sessions, global conferences, trade negotiations and other global meetings. The Center holds consultative status with the Economic and Social Council of the United Nations and has participated in conferences on population, food, women, trade, development, housing, employment and technology.

Probably the Center of Concern has had more impact on U.S. policy at global conferences than any other non-governmental organization (NGO). On many occasions the Center of Concern is asked to critique position papers on the basic issues. During the Conference its staff was in residence and received daily briefings on the status of negotiations. After the Conference the Center held seminars for a wide range of church and other NGOs to interpret the results.

Philip Land, S.J., helped to create an international organization of NGOs in preparation for UNCTAD IV, which has continued until the present. Known as the International Coalition for Development Action (ICDA), its office is in New York. The Reverend Bob Scott, an Anglican priest from New Zealand, serves as Secretary.

The Center of Concern is actively involved in the Interreligious Task Force on U.S. Food Policy. The Director, Peter Henriot, S.J., was the principal author of the major publication, Identifying a Food Policy Agenda for the 1980s: A Working Paper.

The Center of Concern publishes Center Focus which is distributed quarterly to the 15,000 persons on its mailing list. The newsletter gives considerable emphasis to global justice issues. For example, the November 1980 issue dealt primarily with the "Failure of UN Special Session." The article detailed the breakdown of negotiations aimed at providing a framework to guide global negotiations "for the better management of the global economy."

The quote below provides insight into concerns that are central to this organization:

> Fundamentally, this issue is related to the
> ultimate decision-making authority and where
> it would reside, either in a UN central body
> or in the Specialized Agencies such as the
> International Monetary Fund (IMF), the World
> Bank or the agricultural organization (FAO).
> The Group of 77 (G-77) of developing countries
> were proposing that a UN central conference
> located in New York should have the final

authority. This conference or forum would
centralize the decision-making framework and,
by bringing the specialized agencies within
the overall global negotiations, make possible
an integrated approach toward global economic
issues.

The United States, however, insisted that any
central forum must respect the competency and
"integrity of the specialized agencies (read IMF)
and that their present autonomy be maintained.
It may be noted that under the present system
of voting, the U.S. exercises virtual control
over the IMF.... To avoid being isolated,
Washington pressured Bonn, London and Paris
to reject the text also. In the end, Great
Britain and West Germany stood with the United
States. (The vote: 148-3)[7]

In a conference on "Justice Challenges in the 1980s," the Center of
Concern held a "family reunion" for some 30 co-workers, staff and friends in
April 1981, to evaluate the work of the past and plan for the future. One
specific result was the decision to reaffirm the vocation of intellectual
consciousness raising. In the future the effort will be to extend this
ministry beyond the present constituency of Roman Catholic and other religious leaders into a ministry to the laity. To that end a new staff person
is being employed on a full-time basis.

Critical Evaluation of the Center of Concern

The Center of Concern is a small, independent Jesuit-related group of
theologian-social science scholars who educate, provide guidance and influence
policy out of all proportion to its size and budget. The staff is perceptive,
hard-working and intellectually rigorous. While it does not focus especially
on world hunger, the Center makes an outstanding contribution through its
emphasis on global justice. Its international justice efforts are conducted
in the context of support for grass-roots development with an eye to how
every structure and policy has impact on the very poor. It serves as a model
to be emulated by others in its decision to follow closely the North-South
dialogue and to try to influence the emerging structures of the new international economic order.

A Society of Holy Cross Forum on World Hunger

The third room to be explored (briefly) is a forum sponsored by the
Justice and Peace Center, Society of Holy Cross, Notre Dame, Indiana in 1975.
It is chosen as a sample of how sincere people in religious orders have
grappled with world hunger without having the expertise to get to the basic
issues.

The three-day meeting featured 18 papers presented by respected religious leaders, most within the Society of Holy Cross. In the keynote address Reverend Theodore M. Hesburgh sketched the links of interdependence which he termed a modern Copernican revolution:

> This new look is a fallout of the Space Age...
> a new look at the world from afar. There it
> whirls in the black void of space, blue and
> brown, flecked with white clouds...

Reverend Hesburgh felt that it is good strategy to focus on food as a way of dealing with the whole range of global problems because of the urgency of this issue in itself, and because people identify better with hunger than with trade, commodity prices or other issues. He decried cuts in PL-480 food aid by five-sixths between 1965-1975, with much of the small remaining portion going to Indonesia, Korea and Israel where political and military considerations dominated.

Of the other 17 speakers only one attempted to deal with systemic causes underlying the problem. All reflected sincerity and concern. Many called for those present to adopt a more severe lifestyle of poverty and greater personal identification with the poor. Much attention was given to cutting down meat consumption and fasting as personal responses. But the conference never dealt with specific issues of trade, commodity prices, corporate policies, IMF policies, grain reserves or any other form of restructuring of the international economic system.

There were many references to the rich taking advantage of the poor. For example, "Too often we are shepherds who eat the flock...we are the problem -- our excessive materialism and selfish interest." But there was little attempt to translate this insight into what happens in the global economic structures.

The Reverend James Kelly, C.S.C., of Moreau Seminary had the right idea when he said, "Find the levers and gears and shift." But those levers and gears were never found in the conference.

One speaker quoted Rollo May's book Love and Will: "The central core of modern man's neurosis, it may be fairly said, is the undermining of the experience of himself as responsible, the sapping of his will and ability to make decisions." But this conference itself substituted personal lifestyle decisions for the large and more difficult public policy decisions that are required to deal with the poverty and hunger of 500 million people.

As one speaker noted, "too many of us resolve the world hunger crisis by turning off the TV set when a program on hunger is presented." Others resolve the problem by taking on personal sacrifice that does not eventuate in solving the problem. Others of us, in good faith, are ready to "leave third world countries to weed their own gardens" to save the poor and hungry from our domination. This is an attractive alternative in that it frees our nation from responsibility and our consciences from guilt, but it is faulty as a policy because global hunger will not go away for the eighth of the world's population that is malnourished and in abject poverty, as long as global structures continue to be patterned in unjust ways.

It was Reverend Reginald McQuaid, C.S.C., who put the issue in proper perspective:

> For the rich countries, no solution is
> acceptable which interferes with the free
> market economy, whereby the rich are free
> to continue to amass wealth through taking
> advantage of the weaker bargaining position
> of the poor.... For the free enterprisers,
> the pursuit of wealth is the basic motivation
> which makes for human progress. The fact
> that it has resulted in the concentration of
> vast economic power in the hands of a few
> families while hundreds of millions are
> starving is to them beside the point.[8]

II. THE LUTHERAN CHURCHES

The hunger program described in this section is coordinated through the Lutheran Council in the USA and represents the work of the American Lutheran Church (ALC), the Lutheran Church in America (LCA), and the Association of Evangelical Lutheran Churches (AELC).

* The American Lutheran Church, headquartered in Minneapolis, Minnesota has 4,800 congregations and 2.4 million members.

* The Lutheran Church in America is headquartered in New York City, has 6,100 congregations and 3 million members in the USA and Canada.

* The Association of Evangelical Lutheran Churches is headquartered in St. Louis, Missouri, has 270 congregations and 110,000 members.

The ALC and the LCA began their hunger programs in 1974. The newly created AELC, which broke from the Missouri Synod Lutheran Church, initiated its hunger appeal last year. In 1980, the Conventions of the ALC and LCA approved extension of their successful hunger programs for six and ten years respectively.

Of the money collected by the AELC, two-thirds is earmarked for global hunger concerns and one-third for domestic hunger. AELC domestic hunger monies are divided between the National Indian Lutheran Board and Bread for the World.

All three hunger programs take their direction either from social statements passed at Conventions or from the advice and counsel of denominational leaders. The overseas money is sent through the cooperative agency, Lutheran World Ministries. LWM, in turn, gives money to Lutheran World

Relief, the overseas development agency of U.S. Lutherans, to the Lutheran World Federation, the international family of Lutheran Churches, which has aid programs in many countries, and to the Ecumenical Development Cooperative Society, which makes loans to development programs of the churches in low income nations.

At the local level, hunger concern is the responsibility of the Social Outreach Committee of local congregations. Once each year there is a special hunger emphasis with an offering. Each congregation sets its own date for this observance; many churches have their appeal during the Thanksgiving season.

American Lutheran Church Hunger Programs

Since 1974 the Hunger Appeal of the ALC has collected $11 million. The 1980 contributions to the Hunger Appeal were for $2,073,000. Last year the ALC gave 84 percent of all hunger offerings overseas. Efforts to educate and mobilize the churches received 7.5 percent.

The stated objectives of the ALC Hunger Program are:

* to increase awareness of ALC members concerning root causes of hunger in the U.S. and in other parts of the world;

* to encourage participation of ALC members in influencing U.S. public policy regarding hunger and poverty throughout the world;

* to assist members in modification of lifestyle toward simpler patterns of consumption;

* to facilitate voluntary sharing of financial resources by members toward the alleviation of hunger worldwide;

* to counsel with members who have special knowledge and experience in the field of hunger and poverty;

* to support the ALC Board of Trustees in an ongoing review of investments in corporations whose activities have impact on the nutrition of people in this country and overseas;

* to work cooperatively with other Lutherans and other religious organizations in hunger education and action.

The ALC has structured its hunger emphasis as an "inter-unit program" with accountability to the ALC General Convention and the Church Council through the Office of Church in Society. A National Hunger Advisory Committee is composed of nine leaders from the major Divisions and Offices of the denomination. Services are offered to the congregations through the Division for Life and Mission in the Congregation. Dr. George S. Johnson serves as the Director for Hunger Ministries and coordinates the Hunger Staff Team. On

the staff are 15 Service Mission Directors and five Parish Support Persons.
On this team, also, is Ms. Kathleen Dougherty, Food Policy Advocate with the
Lutheran Council USA, who heads the Washington office.

A pamphlet on hunger which has wide distribution in ALC churches is
titled "Are There Still Hungry People?" It begins by pointing out that one
in eight persons in the world is malnourished. Crops have been good globally
since 1976 but the poor do not have money to buy food. Much of the pamphlet
deals with hunger in the United States. It then moves to the ALC Hunger
Appeal. Three-fourths of all gifts go overseas. Of the 25 percent used in
this country, half is for U.S. hunger projects and the other half is for
education and an effort to influence legislation, including contributions to
Bread for the World and the Interreligious Task Force on U.S. Food Policy.
The funds that go abroad are used primarily for development projects such
as water conservation, credit for small farmers, agricultural extension
education, granaries, or roads to get grain to markets.

Lutheran Church in America Hunger Programs

In the LCA, 10 percent of the $23 million received for hunger programs
since 1974 has gone for direct relief during times of famine or catastrophe,
72 percent has gone into overseas development projects, 15 percent for
education and advocacy, and 3 percent for administration.

LCA publishes a bimonthly newsletter, LCA Hunger Appeal. Part of the
space lists offerings received and urges more giving. Another section
describes the use of funds in development projects. A typical aid project
is in the village of Niang M'Boul, Mauritania. The 100 people in the village
had fallen on hard times because of drought. A local resident secured an old
rusted pump and brought water to the village so that small vegetable gardens
could grow. Then Lutheran World Service provided a new three-cylinder pump,
as well as hand tools, seed and fertilizer. The villagers organized a co-op
and began leveling land and digging irrigation channels. This year the
project has been enlarged from seven hectares to 15 hectares (one hectare
equals 2.5 acres). The church is now trying to teach good money management
so that funds will be available for repair and replacement of the pump.

The remainder of the newsletter is devoted to "Legislative Update."
In a typical issue three topics were discussed -- Project North, a Canadian
effort to help the cause of Native justice, a brief statement on the vote at
WHO on the Infant Formula Marketing Code, and a brief paragraph on the Reagan
Administration's plan to shift federal funds into block grants.

A pamphlet, used widely in local churches, is titled "Where Are The
Hungry People?" It states in the initial section, "Hunger is potentially the
most explosive spiritual, humanitarian and political problem facing the world
today.... The basic cause of hunger is poverty." The brochure then gives
its analysis of the cause of hunger:

> Massive hunger overseas results not from
> famine, but from the collapse of age-old

agricultural economics in the third world
-- suddenly thrust in competition with
the developed technological economies of
the west. The demise of small-scale
agriculture in these countries, coupled
with their headlong rush toward industrialization, has propelled powerful minorities
into prosperity and left masses prey to
starvation.

The pamphlet quotes from a report of the World Hunger Working Group
which reported to President Carter. The problem of hunger is stated in
terms traditionally understood by farmers:

* Readily arable land is reaching its limits.
* Fresh water supplies are shrinking.
* Energy supplies are dwindling and costly.
* Population growth undermines real growth in
  grain production.
* Land tenure patterns discourage productivity.
* Agricultural research is aimed at cash crops.
* Rural unemployment has caused large numbers
  to move to the cities.

The issues of trade barriers, readjustments in national and international institutions and absence of grain reserves were mentioned in a
sentence.

The final page titled "Advocacy Check List" describes ways to work
for justice -- visit a summer feeding program, write Congressmen, run for
public office, help establish a school lunch program, join Bread for the
World or the IMPACT network, or write a corporation in which one holds stock
to inquire about policies of social responsibility.

Perhaps the most significant action by the LCA in recent times was
the adoption of a social statement on Economic Justice at the tenth Biennial
Convention in Seattle in 1980. The statement does not deal directly with
hunger or global poverty but it does provide a framework in which this
overarching problem can be placed. The statement should provide denominational leaders with a stronger base of support for dealing with the systemic
causes underlying hunger. In the introduction the LCA said:

God commands that persons deal equitably and
compassionately in their use of the earth's
limited resources in order to sustain and
fulfill the lives of others.

In the section on "Justice" the term is defined as "distributive
love.... It is what God's love does when many neighbors must be served with
limited resources."

The statement supports participatory decision-making in every society. It states that the poor should be "co-determiners of the quality of their economic life.... A society is healthier when its members are encouraged to participate responsibly."

The groundwork is laid for a broader amd more profound level of analysis and criticism of the existing social order. Those who feel called to work at the level of systemic issues should be supported. The statement says, "The criticism and reshaping of economic relations and institutions is a fundamentally moral task in which Christians should be actively involved."

An Implementing Resolution calls upon ministers and congregations to engage in intensive study over the next two years. Further, it directs program agencies and offices to do the same. The Staff Team on World Hunger Concerns is singled out by name as an official group to whom this mandate applies. Finally, the mandate states:

> The Division for Mission in North America, through
> its program, Advocacy for Social Justice, shall
> identify and act upon the global and domestic
> implications of the statement as they impinge on
> the reality of world hunger.

Cooperative Activities

Hope for a Hungry World, written by Charles P. Lutz, was prepared by the Missouri Synod Lutherans and is used also by ALC and LCA through "The Coordinating Committee for Cooperative Parish Education Projects." This kit has served as a primary educational tool and study course in the churches.

The course has two purposes: (1) to show that world hunger is caused by human error, greed, and sin, not from any inadequacy on the part of the Creator, and (2) to lead those who study to move beyond a shallow response of charity to a primary concern for justice.

Basic causes of hunger, as described in the leader's guide, are: (1) Americans eat too much; (2) rich nations buy grain leaving little for poor nations; and (3) not enough help has been given to poor nations for them to buy or grow more grain.

One session deals with inequities in the international system. The low price of bananas paid the exporting country is compared to high prices in U.S. retail stores. The other example shows how in 1960 Malaysia could buy six tractors for 25 tons of rubber, but in 1975 the same rubber bought only two tractors. The chapter mentions commodity agreements and debt relief for poor countries. It ends by asking whether American Christians would be willing to accept a lower standard of living to help the poorest people of the world.

The material includes some excellent quotations from political leaders, economists and church leaders. The only mention of the Group of 77 is in a quote from the material of John V. Taylor, Anglican Bishop of Winchester, "So, in the long run it may be better for us all when the poorer nations begin to organize and dictate their own terms."[9]

The other cooperative educational program that has been used widely for the past six years is designed for a more select audience and is called "Listening to People" conferences. These are sponsored by the Division for Mission in North America and are held in churches of both LCA and ALC as part of the World Hunger/Advocacy Program. Findings of the conferences are written in brochure form and distributed throughout the churches. Essentially, the conferences are ways for rural Lutherans to think through their views as Christians and to express them to the churches at large.

One series of meetings was held for high school students. The conferences focused on nutrition education, food at home and school, domestic food needs and world hunger needs. After discussing junk foods, school lunches and church dinners, the final topic was global hunger. The world is divided, according to the findings, into three groups -- those without enough food, those with barely enough, and those with too much. Students felt that American consumption was habitual rather than intentional and could be corrected by education and personal commitment. The only reference to a systemic cause of hunger was a recognition that some multinational agribusiness corporations are powerful forces in perpetuating hunger in developing countries through buying large tracts of land and growing crops for export. Young people were urged to respond by joining Bread for the World and by sending money to Lutheran World Relief.

Another type of consultation brought together farmers and consumers to discuss the perspective of each group. Others dealt with the preservation of the family farm, land use policies in the USA, and food and energy, with a discussion of who should decide the level of farm production and how farmers should be protected from lowered prices of their products.

The final "Listening to People" consultation mentioned was held in Kansas City in March 1977 for 75 persons on the subject of grain reserves. The statement which resulted from the conference said:

> We are United States farmers. We are
> Christians concerned that the food we
> grow be part of healing a hungry world.
> We want our country to be a sign of
> hope in that world. We wish to share
> both our food and our hope in ways
> which will get food to people without
> reducing their dignity and give all
> farmers a fair return on their labor
> and investment.

The conferees agreed that reserves should not be used as a disincentive to food production within the developing countries, they must reach the neediest people, and U.S. reserves should become part of an international system. Greater stress should be placed on helping developing nations to become more self-reliant in food production. The Conference concluded that storage of grain should be done close to the area of production, but some might be stored in developing countries. FAO should be responsible for establishing specific criteria and timing for release of grain for emergency use.

Finally, it will be helpful to look at a recent statememt made by the Board of Directors of Lutheran World Relief as it relates to public policy on world hunger. The resolution, adopted by LWR on December 16, 1980 sets food aid in global perspective. It (a) reaffirms LWR commitment to respond to human need and work for elimination of hunger and poverty; (b) reasserts that U.S. government policies and programs that meet human need are in the essential interest of the United States as part of an interdependent world; (c) understands that meeting basic human need on a global scale contributes to the national security of the United States; (d) calls on Lutheran churches to foster increased awareness of interdependence and to stimulate members to become more active advocates for U.S. policies that alleviate hunger and promote social and economic justice; (e) recognizes the need of governments to restructure international relations and national priorities to facilitate the abolition of hunger and poverty; and (f) pledges to keep under continuing review the relevance of global issues to LWR and to continue discussions of the global economic perspective.

In Washington, lobbying by the Lutheran Council in the USA is done by Ms. Kathleen Dougherty who holds the position of Food Policy Advocate. Ms. Dougherty has been in the position for a year but was new to food issues and to Washington when she came to the job. She serves on the domestic food committee at the Interreligious Task Force. She arranged recently for testimony before a House Committee on Food Stamps, but to date has limited most of her activities to domestic matters. Additional lobbying is done by Larry Minear and Carol Capps whose salaries are paid partly by Church World Service and partly by the Lutheran Churches.

An Evaluation

The Lutheran denominations are working cooperatively on issues related to world hunger. Their annual emphasis has been extended by formal Convention votes for six and ten years, longer than any other major denominations. The Lutheran World Relief program is considered to be well administered and effective with the major emphasis on development projects similar in character to those supported by other denominations.

There is very little critical analysis of systemic causes underlying world poverty in the Lutheran literature. Much of what is written seems to be directed toward farm families and reflects their traditional perspective. The material is useful but it does not get to a fundamental level. When systemic causes are stated, there is inadequate explanation to help the uninformed get a real grasp of the issues and what the United States can do about them.

The "Listening to People" conferences are good in giving people a chance to meet together, reflect on issues of concern to them and express their views to others in the churches. They are weak in input from specialists who understand the issues of the international economic order, or even the issues of injustice within developing societies. The prophetic note seems to be missing.

The statement by the LCA on "Economic Justice" is a splendid abstract philosophical and theological treatise from a Lutheran perspective. It avoids any application of principles to real situations, leaving the reader to draw whatever implications are to be found. The statement is being widely discussed throughout the churches, and with proper guidance, could form the rationale for a more substantive approach to the issues.

Finally, the recent statement by Lutheran World Relief is cast in very general terms. While making a contribution on broad principles, it fails to provide any guidance on specific issues which would be controversial.

The hunger programs in the Lutheran Churches appear to be firmly under the control of denominational leaders who are compassionate and concerned for a hungry world but who do not allow the prophetic word to be spoken except in statements of broad principles.

III.   UNITED METHODIST CHURCH

The United Methodist Church is the largest ecumenically-oriented Protestant denomination and one of the most active and imaginative in its global outreach and emphasis on social justice. Its ministries are divided into major Boards and Commissions which receive most of their funding through the "World Service" budget. Total budget outlays through this channel for 1981 are $28,452,000.

The General Board of Global Ministries received 48 percent of the total. This Board has six large Divisions, five of which are involved with hunger issues. As examples, the Women's Division is concerned with the family-size farm in the United States. The World Division has various types of Agricultural Missionaries and projects. The United Methodist Committee on Relief Division (UMCOR) administers relief, rehabilitation, refugee and small-scale development programs.

Other Boards which receive funds from the "World Service" budget are the General Board of Discipleship which receives 13.76 percent of the funds and has a program dealing with alternate lifestyles, and the Board of Higher Education and Ministry which receives 10.69 percent. It raises the question of what the university can contribute to food production and an end to global poverty. United Methodist Communications gets 9.64 percent of the budget and assists in telling the story about world hunger to Methodists and to the general public. Among the smaller Commissions is the General Board of Church and Society which receives 3.74 percent of the total, or $990,000.

During the quadrennium from 1976 to 1980, "hunger" was a missional priority and was mandated by the General Conference to be emphasized throughout the church. Thirteen million dollars were raised for world hunger as an advance offering, with the money distributed through a coordinating committee. The General Board of Church and Society, which is the primary body dealing with systemic issues, received 18 percent of the total funds.

The current quadrennium is placing special emphasis on the "Peace with Justice Program." The financial support depends upon the amount raised through the World Service Special Gifts. The program is administered through the General Board of Church and Society.

Although the major emphasis is on world peace and justice during this quadrennium, the church will continue its program on world hunger, recognizing that this problem must not be forgotten. This quadrennium the "World Hunger... Special Program" has been placed within the General Board of Global Ministries under the United Methodist committee on Relief Division. Again, the funds are divided broadly among various Boards, with 18 percent of the total to be received by the General Board of Church and Society. The church is anticipating a total of $4 million per year for hunger over this period.

United Methodist Committee on Relief (UMCOR)

During and following World War II, UMCOR functioned as a relief agency, providing food and clothing to victims of war and other disaster. UMCOR estimates that it actually helps some 5.5 million people in 57 countries annually through a variety of programs. In its literature, UMCOR advertises that Methodists are part of an interdependent world and that their gifts are joined with those of many other groups in saying to people in desperate need "You are not alone! We care! We care!" The total funds disbursed by UMCOR amount to more than $8,000,000 annually, and the hunger emphasis adds to that total.

At present the budget of UMCOR is divided as follows:

* Rehabilitation - projects up to three years........44%
* Relief - short term, capacity to respond
    within hours of a disaster.....................20%
* Refugees - including settlement in the USA.........10%
* Renewal of Life - development projects of more
    than three years duration......................16%
* Other - including overhead costs..................10%

One-third of UMCOR's work is done directly through United Methodist Church channels, while two-thirds is done ecumenically. The three channels for ecumenically-related projects are the Commission of Inter-Church Aid, Refugee and World Service of the World Council of Churches, and Church World Service, which received 25 to 30 percent of its funding from UMCOR.

Of special interest are the development projects, termed "Renewal of Life" projects. The approach is to help people develop their own programs, so that health care is not _for_ people but _by_ people in need. The projects are relatively small-scale, are mostly in rural areas, and they offer the promise of helping discrete groups of people to help themselves. Projects usually fall into one of these categories:

* Community development programs
* Training of rural leadership
* Expansion of water resources
* Revolving fertilizer banks
* Agricultural technology
* Credit programs for farmers
* Planned parenthood programs

Each project is described in the Partnership in Mission Catalog, and local churches or Districts can take an entire project or share one with another group. The projects may range in cost from a few thousand dollars a year to $100,000 or more.

The Board of Church and Society

The Board of Church and Society receives more than $1 million annually for its regular program. During the quadrennium from 1976 to 1980 it received over $2 million in additional funds for use in the world hunger emphasis. The emphasis of this Board is on public policy and systemic causes of injustice in society.

The Board of Church and Society was created by the General Conference. There are 92 persons on this Board, one from each Annual Conference. The Board of Church and Society is organized into five departments and a number of Task Forces and Committees. The Departments are Human Welfare, Political and Human Rights, Peace and World Order, Social and Economic Justice, and Environmental Justice and Survival. One of the Task Forces is Peace with Justice, and another is the World Hunger Consultation Task Force.

The Department that deals most directly with justice in the international economic order is the Department of Peace and World Order. This Department's concerns include UN affairs, disarmament, U.S. foreign policy including tariffs and trade, U.S. military policy, transnational corporations, and international development.

The Board has a building in New York which is used by the Department of World Peace and Justice and is directed by Dr. Robert McClean. This office monitors UN policy debates, deals with the UN Development Program, and offers continuing education programs about the work of the Group of 77 and other issues before the United Nations. A major project is the Global Negotiations Information Project. The bi-weekly newsletter is the most extensively used material available on Global Negotiations to both individuals and governments. The United Methodists have kept this project alive and fostered its further development through the use of hunger funds from the Advance Special.

Engage/Social Action (E/SA)

E/SA is published 11 times annually and is used by pastors and churches, with a circulation of more than 10,000. Of course, the magazine covers the whole range of social justice issues that are concerns of the Divisions within Church and Society. Our question is how well E/SA has addressed systemic issues underlying world hunger.

An editorial in the July/August 1981 issue of E/SA titled "Reflections" is based on the phrase, "We hold government responsible...," a phrase from the United Methodist Social Principles. The editorial dealt with domestic concerns, but the principle evoked applies as well to the issue of a just global economy. The editorial was a reflection on how the present administration plans to dismantle social programs aimed at helping the poor. It condemned the suggestion that the churches should provide these humanitarian services. The article concluded that churches will increase their social service programs, but it should be understood that there is no way churches can meet the need in the magnitude that is required, nor should they. This is a responsibility of society at large.

A special issue of E/SA was titled "Justice in a Hungry World" and reached a total circulation of 200,000. The special issue had a series of articles on various aspects of world hunger. The article most relevant to our concern was titled, "The Systemic Roots of Hunger" by Norman J. Faramelli. The article focused on six systemic causes of world hunger:

1. The pattern of development. Development has followed the model of the United States and focused on industrial development to the neglect of appropriate agricultural development. Efforts to improve agriculture frequently concentrate on large-scale farming, with the result that millions of displaced persons move to the slums of the cities where they cannot find work.

The proposed solution is to help the poor who live on the land to find small-scale appropriate technology so they can grow wheat to make their own bread and then keep the food they have grown, rather than have it sold elsewhere by an absentee landlord. Yet there is recognition of the need for a balanced industrial development that provides jobs for the needy.

2. Overpopulation. While some say that overpopulation is the root cause of hunger, others feel that it is the result of hunger and poverty. Studies conducted in five states in India showed that population growth rates were substantially reduced only after the children had proper food and medical care, after some form of Social Security was provided, and when women were given options other than child bearing. Nevertheless, vigorous birth control programs need to accompany these other changes.

3. Aid and trade: Help or hindrance? The way aid has been used, the author concluded, has done as much harm as good, although there does need to be a transfer of resources from rich to poor. U.S. aid has so many strings attached that it has become a subsidy for U.S. exports. PL-480 sends food to political friends more than to the needy; it is primarily a weapon in the foreign policy arsenal.

Similarly, expanding trade has not always helped poor nations. Between 1970 and 1974 in East Africa, for example, export prices rose 34 percent but import prices rose 91 percent. The author recognized the argument of those who propose a radical self-sufficiency, moving away from all trade, but believed that in the real world this is not an option; the answer lies in more favorable terms of trade to poor nations.

4. <u>Arms madness.</u> In this section the writer developed the thesis that sale of armaments is out of control, and that the cost should be used for development that overcomes poverty and hunger.

5. <u>Grain reserves.</u> Any plan to start feeding the hungry of the world requires a system of international grain reserves. Beginning with national reserves is a step in the right direction.

6. <u>Weather.</u> Changing weather conditions may increase the uncertainty of famine and therefore contribute to world hunger.

Church and Society also sends Methodist leaders packets of materials mailed on a regular basis from the Board's headquarters in Washington, D.C. with current information on national legislation that needs citizen action, upcoming issues, and suggestions for action.

The two buildings at 100-110 Maryland Avenue, S.E. in Washington, D.C. and the New York building at 777 UN Plaza provide structural symbols of the United Methodists' concern for peace and social justice.

An Evaluation

The United Methodist Church is the beneficiary of persons of vision over the past 50 years who made the case for the social side of the gospel and won battles that many denominations were afraid to fight. The Boards, denominational executives, and pastors can stand more securely for justice in the world social order because consistently the General Conference has adopted statements on these issues that are comprehensive and prophetic.

This denomination makes strong financial appeals and raises large amounts of money for use in meeting world hunger needs. The hunger emphasis is continuing, with more funds available for dealing with systemic causes underlying world hunger than any other denomination can command.

The Methodists are one of a very few denominations who are taking seriously the global negotiations for a new international economic order. The <u>Global Negotiation Action Notes</u> provide a well-written newsletter which gives a running account of meetings and forces at work for or against the new order. This denomination is largely underwriting the cost of the project "because we feel the international economic structure and the search for more just and equitable economic systems is the key to the systemic causes of hunger and poverty."[10]

The magazine <u>Engage/Social Action (E/SA)</u> is well written and deals with many issues related to global hunger. However, the articles are not as clearly focused on the international economic structure and global negotiations as would be helpful. The special issue with 200,000 copies distributed was not as strong on the central issues as might have been expected.

The United Methodist Church is a major donor to the Interreligious Task Force on U.S. Food Policy. It provides from 25-30 percent of the funds of Church World Service and is a major contributor to the Roman Catholic organization, Center of Concern. This same church provides a large share of the funds for the Churches' Center for Theology and Public Policy, and underwrote the cost of this study.

At the General Conference in Portland, Oregon in 1976 the church noted that:

> ...a missing factor is a strong American constituency that favors the sharing of power and the transfer of resources to the developing world.

The statement noted a public opinion survey conducted in 1975 by the Overseas Development Council in which only a few persons said they looked to their church for information on the subject of worldwide poverty. It noted that those without religious affiliation were as sympathetic to the global poor as were practicing Christians and Jews. The General Conference concluded:

> This survey has identified a weakness in American churches. Greater emphasis is needed in liturgy, education, sermons and church media...in order to organize a constituency whose voices would be heard by the government.

That constituency five years later is still small and weak as compared to forces in American society that are moving in the opposite direction. The United Methodist Church is reminded of the words of the Apostle Paul, "Do not become weary in well-doing."

IV.   THE EPISCOPAL CHURCH

The Presiding Bishop's Fund

The Presiding Bishop's Fund for World Relief is the official channel of the Episcopal Church for responding to human need around the world. It was founded in 1940 as an agency to help refugees from Nazi Germany, and was reconstituted after the War in 1947 in its present basic form. Over the years the fund has broadened its scope to respond to disasters, rehabilitation efforts, and educational and development work.

The program is divided into four areas and grants are made from the Fund in each of them for specific projects:

1. Relief. This is crisis response -- immediate help in the wake of war, famine, drought or other disaster. At present the Church is working in Indochina, Cuba, Haiti and Somalia.

2. Rehabilitation. After immediate relief efforts are ended there is a process of rebuilding, usually for a two-year period following a disaster.

3. <u>Refugee resettlement and migration affairs.</u> This is a specialized part of rehabilitation and includes the settlement of refugees in the United States.

4. <u>Short-term development.</u> Projects help to deal with localized causes of hunger and deprivation. The projects include better farming practices, nutrition education programs, literacy and hygiene programs, legal assistance for food stamps and land rights; food-for-work projects, well-digging systems, etc.

The World Hunger Emphasis

The major emphasis on world hunger began in 1975 when a group of concerned Episcopal priests and laypersons, led by Mr. Norman Faramelli (Board Member, Bread for the World), went to see Presiding Bishop John M. Allin and recommended that an office be established to study underlying causes of world hunger and to enlist participation within the Church to help meet human need in the area of hunger.

From this initiative came a resolution adopted in 1976 at the General Convention in Minneapolis which established the Office for Hunger as an official part of the Church. The Reverend Charles A. Cesaretti became the first staff Director. His mandate was to develop a network of concerned persons throughout the Episcopal Church and to produce educational materials and grass-roots involvement.

A National Hunger Committee serves as a Board with one representative from each of the nine Provinces (regions) of the Episcopal Church. In addition, there is one member from the House of Bishops, one from the Executive Council and one at large. There is a Provincial Coordinator in each region of the nation. The National Hunger Committee meets semi-annually, reviews programs and gives direction to the Office. The organization is developed down to the diocese level, with most dioceses having an organized "Hunger Task Force."

The Hunger Office seeks to make its impact on the entire Church. At the last General Convention in Denver, there was a consciousness-raising concert given by John Denver. The organization raises funds in local parishes and now contributes $500,000 annually toward the Presiding Bishop's Fund for World Relief, which now has an annual budget of $3,000,000.

A Review of World Hunger Literature

Dr. David Crean, who became Director of the Hunger Office in 1980, has provided dynamic leadership for the World Hunger movement. There are now 4,500 persons in this "network" of the hunger program. A newsletter goes regularly to these persons with ten issues per year. During Lent in 1979, a study book was prepared for use in parishes, titled Let It Begin With Me, and was used in almost half of the parishes nationwide. Since 1979 there has been a series of publications known as the "Jubilee Series." These books are related to world poverty, hunger and development. The one last year was on energy use, and the one for 1981 relates to land use.

Hunger Notes, the newsletter, is published by the World Hunger Education Fund, with four additional pages of notes written by David Crean for the network. Dr. Pat Kutzner is editor of the main body of the newsletter. In reviewing Hunger Notes and special Hunger Reports, one is impressed with the liveliness and wide-ranging concerns. Earlier issues presented the message indirectly by use of news stories on what individuals were doing or saying. For example, in an early issue, one article described a course taught by the Reverend Stephen K. Commins at the University of California at Los Angeles, "The Politics of Food." The article discussed how the "Green Revolution" is benefitting the affluent in most countries rather than the poor. The professor took the position that in El Salvador the goal of those in power is not to keep the poor tied to the land, but to keep them powerless. Another article was written by a high school student intern in a Hunger Task Force Project sponsored by the Diocese of St. Louis. Participants lived among the very poor in southeast Missouri. The article provided an insight into the harshness of life and the tremendous problems of the poor as seen through the eyes of this intern. Another article described the need for urgent food and medical supplies in Nicaragua. It stated that the Presiding Bishop's Fund sent $28,000 for emergency relief and rehabilitation work and invited groups to send special offerings marked for this work.

Since Dr. David Crean assumed leadership of the Office, there appears to be a shift in emphasis toward presentations of underlying causes of hunger, while still keeping lively stories that appeal directly to the interest and sympathy of readers. A special issue, published shortly after Dr. Crean assumed office, was titled Roots of Hunger. In an introduction, Dr. Crean explained his approach to getting people to deal with the problem. He began with a note of realism:

> Hunger is thus a subtle, insidious and
> vicious killer. Hunger is a fact of modern
> living that is an affront to the sensibilities
> of any thinking, compassionate human being.
> And yet, hunger is a phenomenon with which
> we are unable or unwilling to grapple in a
> profound way.

Dr. Crean presented case studies from four parts of the world, including Appalachia, and then tried to determine the specific causes of hunger in each case. Then he discussed general causes of hunger. His themes in this publication were war, population explosion, export cropping, communication (distribution systems), energy, weather, and mission (people impelled by the gospel to help).

While the material was well-written and helpful to the reader, it did not get to the bedrock of forces causing poverty and hunger or identify what can be done to change them. In discussing the weather, for example, the article mentioned drought conditions in the Sahel and overgrazing which denudes the ground cover. But there was no hint as to what is being done to correct the situation, or the kinds of forces that perpetuate the present condition.

One does not detect sparks of hope from the analysis, nor is the Christian guided in what can be done. The author acknowledged his lack of expertise in economics and stated that his professional training is in the food sciences.

However, Dr. David Crean has been a fast learner. He appears to have been influenced significantly by the two major reports of the past year, Overcoming World Hunger: The Challenge Ahead and North-South: A Program for Survival. In Hunger Notes (Vol. 6, No. 4, September 1980) in a front page letter, he urged readers to study these two books. He sensed in the Church "an expanding awareness of the issues impinging upon our central concern -- hunger." He concluded, "We can eliminate hunger. We should eliminate hunger. We must eliminate hunger."

Let It Begin With Me is a well-conceived booklet or guide prepared by the Office for Hunger in 1978 and used as a church-wide study in nearly half the Episcopal parishes in the United States during Lent in 1979. The curriculum was prepared under the direction of the Reverend Scott Paradise, Chaplain of MIT, and formerly of the Boston Industrial Mission. The book is divided into ten sections, each of which presents a theme for use in a session.

The content of the book is a mixture of dealing with hunger "out there" and of "personal response" through fasting, more simple foods, and better shopping information at the supermarket. Its methodology is especially imaginative -- the author is keenly aware of the need to bring his audience into feeling the injustice and apathy that can surround those who are victims of injustice and poverty.

The preface provides a Biblical basis for concern with hunger in stark and poetic language:

"An appeal for food lies nestled in the heart of
The Lord's Prayer."

"At the holiest moment in Christian worship bread
is broken and shared."

"Jesus fed the hungry multitudes."

The preface continues with a statement of the importance of this study and then says, "For Christians it may involve salvation or damnation. For humankind it means life or death."

The second session begins with a meal. Those present are randomly assigned to represent a continent. The affluent continents have large tables, many chairs and are served large portions of tasty food. Those from Asia and Africa are given only rice, bread and tea. A presentation is made of the present situation and future hopes for the peoples of each continent. After discussion of the feelings of various groups toward inequities, the evening ends with an overview of facts about hunger, malnutrition and poverty on a global scale. At each session there are "exercises," simulated games, and the presentation of homework. One session begins with the ending of a 24-hour fast. Another begins with participants having eaten for a week on a welfare income.

In a recent interview with Dr. David Crean, he indicated a keen awareness of the systemic issues of international economic order, but stated that one must be careful how these are presented and promoted in the Church. They are, he stated, "issues that make a lot of people angry." He has also been cautious of being critical of corporations located abroad. His organization did not endorse the Nestle' boycott because it would upset too many constituents, but they did prepare a position paper which explained the reasons for the boycott and, in effect, did lend their support.

Dr. Crean has circulated widely the two major public reports which deal with systemic causes underlying world hunger. He brought together Church leaders in a conference to better understand these issues. He also helped to initiate and provided a good part of the money for a conference at the University of Wisconsin on Church-University cooperation on world hunger issues, which was held in May 1981.

An Evaluation

While appearing to grow in his own understanding of the systemic causes underlying world hunger, and while moving much further in the presentation of these issues than his predecessor, Dr. Crean is aware of the large conservative segment in the Episcopal Church. He appears to be seeking validation for his position and that of the Office of Hunger. A clear statement of systemic forces and the need to deal with them openly and forcefully will probably have to come through a resolution at the next General Convention if the Office is to have the backing that is necessary to move further to the offensive.

The nationwide interest in problems of hunger on the part of members of the Episcopal Church is an impressive expression of concern. The grass-roots organizational network has sustained its interest and has grown steadily since it was organized. David Crean has had access to funds to place in educational projects that have offered promise of getting to important systemic issues. The Office is extremely small -- Dr. Crean and one secretary. It is impossible for him to spend sufficient time in strengthening the network or in developing a comprehensive "alert" system for contacting Congress on key issues.

In summary, the hunger emphasis in the Episcopal Church follows its familiar pattern of establishing a small office and then building a network of concerned persons with the help of the Bishop's staff at the diocese level. The program is vital and growing. It is moving toward dealing with systemic causes of hunger in a more fundamental way. It is to be hoped that the next General Convention will approve a clear statement of the global dimension of the problem and thus provide the staff director with a more solid base. It would seem that a single professional staff person to direct and build a nationwide program for a major denomination is grossly inadequate personpower for the task.

V. PRESBYTERIANS

The United Presbyterian Church USA and the Presbyterian Church in the
U.S. are just completing a merger of their hunger programs. The Presbyterian
Hunger Program (PHP), while a joint venture of the two denominations, still
has two headquarters: one in Atlanta at the denominational offices of the
Presbyterian Church U.S., and the other in New York, the headquarters of the
United Presbyterian Church USA. The Washington Affairs Office of the two
denominations has long been operated cooperatively, with the PCUS representa-
tive being George Chauncey and the UPCUSA staff director being Mary Jane
Patterson.

The Presbyterian Church in the U.S.

It is both interesting and inspiring to read through the minutes of
the General Assemblies of the Presbyterian Church in the U.S. from 1969 to
1981. This denomination, unlike others, began its great emphasis on hunger
issues in 1969 when the General Assembly declared:

> ...that world hunger is so real and grave that
> this problem is a top priority concern of the
> Presbyterian Church of the U.S. and that all
> possible resources for at least the next five
> years must be focused on ways and means of
> dealing with the problem.[11]

At that time a "Task Force on World Hunger" was formed within the
church to encourage all boards and agencies to emphasize hunger-related
issues, and to itself undertake projects which would spur giving and involvement.

By the time other denominations described in this report had started
their programs in 1974, this church had five years of significant experience.
In 1972 the church approved a new plan for an Easter offering. Seventy
percent of the offering was administered by the Board of World Missions, as
in previous years, for relief, rehabilitation and development projects, but
the other 30 percent was to be administered by the Task Force on World Hunger, to be used in "model programs" to combat root causes of hunger at home
and abroad.

In the USA, Task Force funds were used to help rural black farmers
raise better crops through cooperatives, to help in nutrition and economic
education programs in Appalachia, to give counsel and assistance to urban
Indians, and to aid migrant workers. Abroad, the funds assisted creative
agricultural development of landless peasants in northern Brazil, helped in
community development in Haiti, taught employment skills to youth in Kenya,
and provided family planning services in the Philippines.

An especially significant Consultation on World Hunger and Development
was held May 27-31, 1973 at the Georgia Center for Continuing Education. The
meeting brought together 135 leaders from academic circles, business, government, ministers, missionaries, and representatives of developing nations.

The purpose was to marshal "the strength of our church and its membership in attacking root causes of world hunger and promoting development in the third world."

The results of this Consultation became the central feature of a special presentation to the General Assembly later in 1973. The 1974 report indicated that the Consultation had far exceeded expectations.[12] The Church World Service representative described it as a "bellwether" for the American Christian community in response to the crisis of world hunger. At the 1974 meeting, with the food crisis deepening, the church saw both an opportunity and a duty:

* to prick the conscience of our nation to the plight of two-thirds of mankind affected by deepening hunger;
* to use the power of committed citizenship to affect the policies of our government for development aid;
* to urge American-based multinational corporations to give priority to the hungry in their economic relations with developing nations; and
* to convey to hundreds of millions around the world the good news of Christ who has come to establish justice on the earth, to set free those who are oppressed.

In this landmark General Assembly, local churches and presbyteries were asked to carry out educational programs to inform constituents about human needs and relate them to national legislative proposals such as the following:

* Increase American food aid to the 40 poorest countries of the world.
* Increase multilateral rather than bilateral government aid programs.
* Reform U.S. development aid by separating humanitarian aid from military aid.
* Support U.S. participation in building world food reserves.
* Reform U.S. trade policies to permit the import of goods into our markets from third world countries.
* Develop a long-range plan for U.S. participation in a global food aid program.

It is interesting to note that in an addendum to the 1974 report, there was a series of recommendations for a cooperative program with the United Presbyterian Church in the USA on world hunger issues, most of which are finally being implemented in 1981.

The 1975 report described the powerfully significant World Food Conference in 1974 and the surge of interest on the part of American Christians:

> Every major religious body has responded,
> not only with official declarations, but by
> giving this issue top priority in the life and

> mission of their constituency. More than
> that, the issue has called forth ecumenical
> cooperation on a scale unprecedented by any
> such issue in the past.

In 1977 the report "reaffirmed the statement of 1964: "Christians should give their unqualified support to the United Nations in its effort to establish the reign of law in international relations." And in 1979 there was an especially perceptive general statement:

> As Christians, we shall be advocates in
> the centers of political and economic power,
> supporting policy changes which will provide
> food for the poor and hungry people at home and
> abroad, which empower their self-development,
> and which enable them and us by just and peace-
> ful means to be free from oppressive and unjust
> systems that fail to meet basic needs.

Beginning in 1979, the World Service and World Hunger Report to the General Assembly assumed the proportion of a large 16 page booklet. Below is a summary of the 1981 report to the 121st General Assembly.

The program is now divided into three major parts: (1) World Service, with income of $1,000,000 which is used for development projects; (2) World Hunger, with an income of $504,000 to provide resources for programs attacking root causes of hunger at home and abroad, and (3) Crisis Funds to deal with emergency relief and rehabilitation efforts, with total giving of $885,000.

The report highlighted three successes of 1980 of the Interreligious Task Force on U.S. Food Policy: (1) The creation of an emergency grain reserve to backstop the Food for Peace Program; (2) the "human needs" amendment to legislation authorizing additional funds to the IMF; and (3) the restoration of funds during 1980 to the Food Stamp Program which had been in danger of being severely cut. Efforts that failed in 1980 included, "the effort to urge the U.S. to take a more positive stance in relation to the North-South negotiations in the United Nations, looking to a more just international economic order."

The Hunger Action Program reported that in 1980 it had enlisted over 1,000 new PCUS members in the IMPACT network and hundreds of others in Bread for the World.

The United Presbyterian Church in the USA

The United Presbyterian Church in the USA does not operate its own relief, rehabilitation or development programs abroad. Rather, UPCUSA has chosen to work through Church World Service and the Commission of Inter-Church Aid, Refugee and World Service of the World Council of Churches.

Income for the Hunger Program in 1980 was $2,753,000. The funds were received from the following sources:

```
One Great Hour of Sharing (one-third allocation)....$2,001,394
One Great Hour of Sharing (designated)..................88,182
General Giving for Hunger..............................411,172
United Presbyterian Women..............................175,563
Interest Earned in 1980.................................77,037
```

1980 Total Income.......$2,753,140

The expenditure of funds was divided between that spent in the United States and that sent abroad. Funds spent within the United States were as follows:

```
Direct Feeding Projects..............................$193,225
Development Assistance.................................369,350
Education, Public Policy and Life-Style Modification...454,854
```

$1,017,429

Outside the United States where $1,100,000 was given, direct feeding projects received $303,000 and development assistance got $796,000.

In addition, grants of $100,000 were made for "Middle Judicatory Enablement." This money helped to pay expenses for Synod Hunger Coordinators.

Many development project grants in the United States were made through synods, most of them for $10,000 or less. A random example is the Calvary UPC Elderly Nutrition Program in Milwaukee, Wisconsin which received $2,500. The direct feeding program brought elderly inner city persons to the church five days a week where 25,000 meals were served with federal funds. Calvary Church contributed space and staff time.

The national contributions by UPCUSA included:

```
Bread for the World............................$17,000
Interreligious Task Force.......................42,000
ICCT Infant Formula Program.....................20,000
ICCR Agribusiness Project.......................10,000
NCCC Coordinating Committee on Hunger...........15,000
Hunger Notes (World Hunger Education Service)....3,000
```

The UPCUSA has been contributing as much as 20 percent of its funds for education and public policy advocacy and is considering moving this percentage to 25 percent, depending upon agreements made in the merger process, which is still underway. This denomination, more than most, has evolved from thinking about direct aid to the hungry toward getting at systemic causes underlying hunger and poverty.

The UPCUSA has a two-sided education program. Social Ministries Institutes are held across the country on varying themes, often related to world hunger issues. Dieter Hessel in the New York office is generally responsible for these Institutes. Also, there is the Lifestyle Change Project led by George Wilson which has relevance to world hunger education. Often these institutes are held by synods, with one or two persons from each local church in attendance.

The Presbyterian Hunger Program -- A Joint Venture

This joint venture is still new, and a great deal of staff time for the past year has been directed toward meshing the two denominational programs into one. The strategy for grass-roots involvement is to build and utilize a network of Hunger Action Enablers in the synods and presbyteries of both groups. The program seeks:

> ...to mobilize the human and financial
> resources of the churches to respond with
> justice and compassion to the poor and
> hungry in the local community, in the
> nation, and throughout the world.

PHP is to be financed through portions of the One Great Hour of Sharing Offerings which are designated for hunger by each General Assembly and by year-round giving directly to the Hunger Fund.

The joint program plans to work in five areas:

1. Education. An understanding of what causes hunger in the world is felt to be basic to deciding what must be done. The mandate is both to feed the hungry and loose the bonds of oppression. Two pieces of literature are being circulated and studied: Overcoming World Hunger: The Challenge Ahead (Abridged Edition), and the Presbyterian Hunger Program: Putting the Pieces Together. The latter is a joint publication which provides action ideas and resources for persons or groups studying hunger issues.

2. Direct food relief. The churches are challenged to locate the community-based food programs such as food banks, food stamp programs or meals-on-wheels for those who need these services. Direct food services abroad are, again, channeled through Church World Service and the World Council of Churches.

3. Development assistance. This program provides assistance at a more fundamental level. The kinds of programs sought deal with:

* eroding earth and inadequate water resources;
* farmers using inappropriate methods and laboring on land they never hope to own;
* parents lacking understanding of basic nutrition for their children;
* families too large for their limited resources;
* cities and rural communities lacking adequate health, education and transportation services; and
* producers with inadequate capital and little access to markets.

4. <u>Influencing public policy.</u> The focus for now will be on these issues:

* domestic food assistance programs;
* domestic agricultural policy;
* programs dealing with unemployment;
* economic aid for other nations;
* international trade agreements;
* military spending.

5. <u>Lifestyle integrity.</u> This program studies the implications of six percent of the world's people using 40 percent of the world's food and energy resources. The challenge is for groups within local churches to learn to live more simply and share more fully with those in great need. It also means working for a more just distribution of earth's resources.

The United Presbyterian Church USA is the larger body and has eleven persons on the Coordinating Committee with nine from the PCUS. Generally, the UPCUSA is considered to be the more liberal of the two denominations and traditionally has more freedom for action on systemic causes. However, the PCUS has a long and solid commitment in the field of hunger, and generally its social statements in this field have been both theologically well grounded and far reaching in social vision.

An Evaluation

A number of knowledgeable persons from outside the Presbyterian churches have praised the vision and quality of work of leaders in the hunger programs. George Chauncey (PCUS) has chaired the Interreligious Task Force on U.S. Food Policy from the time of its formation. Perhaps the greatest contribution of this denomination is the effective leadership of this man. Mary Jane Patterson (UPCUSA) is the staff director in the Washington office and works closely with George Chauncey in implementing public policy. Mary Jane Patterson does a large number of seminars annually in which she deals with the new international economic order and does so successfully when she has several days with a group. Ann Nesmith, Hunger Coordinator for UPCUSA and James A. Cogswell, Co-Director for PSUC are also well qualified.

By bringing together the two denominations into one program, the Presbyterians can make a significant impact at the national level. In 1981 this group will be the largest contributor to the Interreligious Task Force on U.S. Food Policy.

The Presbyterians have chosen the ecumenical route for funding programs abroad. This has the advantage of eliminating one competing structure with its attendant overhead costs, and of putting money into programs that are well-established and effective. The disadvantage is that the churches lose the close identity that comes from having their own people responsible for their own programs. Denominational giving is modest in the total amount.

The public policy pronouncements of the PCUS are well stated. Many of the basic causes of global hunger are dealt with regularly. Yet there

rong awareness of the efforts of the Group of 77 and the
United States to changes in the economic order. The state-
c in their generalities, but would be much improved by
re detail the specifics of what is wrong and what needs to

Presbyterian Church USA is contributing $455,000 of a
3 million for education and public policy advocacy, or some
total giving, to this work. This is a much higher percent-
)minations, and is an eminently wise investment in public
tical accountability.

the ..... and development projects within the United States are
scattered and small-scale. If one assumes that these programs are well
managed and useful, one still must say that they do not make much impact on
systemic causes underlying poverty and hunger, although contributions to
rural cooperatives, work with migrants, and educational programs on nutrition,
etc., have their important place.

The public policy issues that are to be the focus of attention for
the new joint effort include economic aid for other nations, international
trade agreements, and excessive military spending. One longs for the clear
prophetic witness sounded by the PCUS in 1969 at the 109th General Assembly.
That document harks back to Ezekiel 33 and describes the prophet's role as
that of a watchman over the household of Israel. He is stationed on the wall
of the city to look for the coming of enemy soldiers. When danger threatens
he blows his trumpet in warning. If he blows his trumpet and nobody listens,
he has done his duty. But if he does not blow the trumpet when danger
threatens, he is responsible for those who die. The statement then adds:

> In the face of 500 million malnourished
> people in abject poverty, it is the prophetic
> role of the church to blow the trumpet.
> Hunger is the world's most deadly curable
> disease. Unlike some other deadly diseases,
> this one has a known cure: food.

VI. BREAD FOR THE WORLD

Bread for the World is a grass-roots Christian laypersons' organization with membership covering the spectrum from evangelicals to "mainline"
Protestants to Roman Catholics. On June 1, 1981 the organization had 37,471
dues-paying members, up from 30,791 when the year began, with a goal of
45,000 by the end of 1981.

BREAD'S purpose is to work with others for the elimination of hunger
everywhere in the world. It works closely with the Task Force on U.S. Food
Policy and others in the formulation and implementation of U.S. policy in
every area that bears on world hunger.

Bread for the World began after Arthur and Paul Simon published a
book in 1973, The Politics of World Hunger.[13] Paul is now a U.S. Congressman

from southern Illinois, and Arthur is President of Bread for the World. Before founding the food organization, Arthur was for 12 years the minister at Trinity Lutheran Church on the lower east side of Manhattan.

The 1981 Annual Report describes how members are organized for Congressional action. There are now 373 State and Congressional District Coordinators, 80 quickline telephone network directors, and 600 other resource persons, all of whom serve without pay. A measure of earlier political clout was demonstrated by passage in both the House and Senate of the "Right to Food" resolution in 1976. Before the resolution was enacted, 240,000 letters and telegrams were sent, the most ever received in Congress except over the Panama Canal treaty. This nationwide effort was sponsored and coordinated by BREAD.

The grass-roots quality of this movement is demonstrated by its sources of income. More than half the budget for 1980 came from memberships and contributions of under $100 -- for a total of $583,375. Contributions of $100 or more amounted to $281,554 with a total income of $1,028,369.

Most of the 35 staff people work in New York at the national headquarters, but four or five are located in the Washington office on Capitol Hill. Staff is paid according to need, with the average salary around $16,000.

A tax-exempt sister organization, Bread for the World Education Fund, has the same Board of Directors and is responsible for research, writing and training. Last year they trained 1,000 persons in how to conduct study groups and community forums on the Presidential Commission's report. Hundreds of meetings on this subject used study guides prepared by the Fund. It also provides study materials for young people and holds conferences on college and seminary campuses in all parts of the nation.

Publications and an Official Policy Statement

Every month Bread for the World sends its 37,000 members a four-page newsletter which describes pending legislation on issues of priority. The BREAD position is stated along with the rationale, and members are told how to contact their Congressmen. There is often, in addition, a background paper on a topic related to world hunger.

From time to time there are longer in-depth background studies which are distributed to members. The book Bread for the World by Arthur Simon is distributed widely. There are also three filmstrips -- one, a general presentation of the purposes, organization, and achievements of BREAD; two, a review of public policy issues; and three, a nuts and bolts filmstrip on how to organize a group locally.

The only official policy statement was issued as Background Paper #4 in 1975. BREAD recognizes the need to update this statement but has not yet done so. However, according to Barbara Howell of the Washington office, the nine areas covered are still important to the organization, with the emphasis shifting, depending upon a reading of current events and legislative proposals.

The 1975 statement begins with a theological rationale:

> By creating us and redeeming us through Jesus
> Christ, He has given us a love that will not
> turn aside from those who lack daily bread....
> As Christians, we affirm the right to food; the
> right of every man, woman and child on earth to
> a nutritionally adequate diet. This right is
> grounded in the value God places on human life.

After affirming the proper role of the church in emergency relief and rehabilitation efforts, the report suggests the need to think in terms of long-range strategies that deal with the causes of hunger. While affirming the value of small-scale development projects sponsored by the churches, it states, "The extent of hunger makes large-scale government assistance essential." The report also recognized that hunger for some is rooted in special privilege for others.

The areas of greatest significance for Bread for the World were listed and discussed. They are:

* An end to hunger in the United States,
* a U.S. food policy committed to world food security and rural development as proposed by the World Food Conference,
* the separation of development assistance from all forms of military assistance,
* trade preferences for the poorest nations,
* reduced military spending,
* study and appropriate control over multinational corporations in developing countries, particularly agribusiness,
* efforts to deal with population growth, and
* encouraging more appropriate patterns of eating and living for American Christians.

In reviewing the popular tracts and brochures of BREAD, one notes that the public policy dimension is always prominent. One statement put the strategy clearly, "Recognizing the crucial nature of public policies to the task of overcoming hunger, Christians are using their citizenship to influence those policies for the benefit of hungry people."

Current Legislative Initiatives

In the early years of BREAD, legislative efforts were aimed more at getting increased funding for foreign assistance than for how to reform the agency responsible for development and food aid. Now BREAD is alert to all legislation that affects American food policy. Much time is spent in studying bills that are being introduced and in lobbying for or against them. But BREAD has its own agenda and is working aggressively to enact its own proposals into federal law.

During 1980 two Congressional victories for the hungry came directly as a result of BREAD efforts. One occurred late in the year, when Congress passed a four-million-ton emergency wheat reserve program valued at more than $700 million. This amount of wheat in a special PL-480 reserve can feed about 20 million people for a year.

The second legislative victory was an odd amendment that cut $100 million in spending on government furniture and used $42.8 million of this saving for emergency food aid to Cambodia and East Africa.

A great deal of effort is expended in seeking to get AID to use funds according to New Directions legislation of 1973, which states that the primary goal of aid is to meet basic human needs in a direct way. At this time, BREAD is working to make the legislative language more detailed, with the intention of then filing a suit in court against AID, if necessary, for not following the legislative mandate.

BREAD recognizes that AID needs to spend part of its funds on projects such as roads, electrical supply systems, and advanced training for elites as indirect ways of helping the poor in the long term. However, BREAD proposes that at least half of the funds should support projects that offer some direct assistance to the poorest. Yet, their analysis indicates that in 1980-81, AID supported three of the former types of projects for every one with some direct aid that meets basic human needs.

Another current legislative initiative of BREAD is an amendment which has been included in the current Food Stamp Bill to set up nutrition monitoring programs. The objective is to determine whether, in fact, the poor who are losing food stamp assistance are becoming malnourished as a result. But the long-term interest is to use this nutrition monitoring program as a pilot, with the hope of learning from it in order to establish similar programs on a worldwide scale. BREAD is working closely with the Institute on Nutrition in Calle, Columbia in an effort to determine how best to fortify food, and to gather data on nutritional deficiencies that can be targeted and corrected.

BREAD is seeking to educate its membership and Congress on the long-term benefits of permitting fledgling industries in third world countries to export manufactured goods to the United States without tariffs. They support a compromise bill which stipulates that when the manufacturing strength of a country reaches a specified level, the free import policy will no longer be in effect.

The largest and most comprehensive legislative initiative of Bread for the World is the Hunger and Global Security Bill, written by BREAD and introduced in this session of Congress. The bill has made surprising progress through the legislative process. In general terms, the bill supports the recommendations of the Presidential Commission on World Hunger and proposes specific legislation to end world hunger and improve global food security. There are five parts to the bill. It would: (1) make the elimination of hunger the primary focus of U.S. relationships with developing countries; (2) urge reassessment of our approach to global security in the light of the destabilizing effects of hunger and poverty; (3) provide U.S. development assistance only to countries that are specifically committed to overcoming hunger and poverty; (4) offer trade advantages to such countries; and (5) press for food security measures, such as an international fund from which countries could borrow when they are faced with a food shortage.

Some of the specific parts of the bill deal with:

1. Title I of Food for Peace. The law now provides for sale of grain at concessionary prices with very low interest and a long repayment period with no strings attached. Title III provides for grants of food but stipulates that it must be used for "self-help" projects in which at least part of the pay is in food. Since most governments prefer Title I and since much of the grain never gets to the people who are most malnourished, this bill stipulates that Title I food should also be targeted to the poorest part of the population and the application should include plans for self-help programs.

2. Direct funds from multilateral lending institutions to poor within countries. The U.S. Department of the Treasury urged the Inter-American Development Bank to establish a policy whereby low income groups benefit directly from at least half of its loans. The measure passed and is now official policy. BREAD now proposes that the World Bank, the Asian Development Bank and the African Development Fund, all of which are beneficiaries of American funds, be asked by the United States to adopt a policy similar to that of the Inter-American Bank. The stakes are very high at the World Bank, where currently $12 billion is loaned annually, and where the amount may be increased substantially. At the $12 billion level of lending, a one percentage point shift in bank lending policy to target direct benefits for the poor means an extra $120 million for them.

3. Special health program within Foreign Assistance Bill. Another section establishes a special health fund within AID and stipulates that it be administered by private voluntary organizations. This fund would be used for programs in areas of the world where a large percentage of children die before age five, and where the average life expectancy is at least 20 years less than in industrialized countries.

4. Grain reserves. Another section of the bill seeks to establish a larger grain reserve program for global security, based on the conclusion of FAO that an amount equal to 18 percent of annual consumption should be in reserve. The bill prohibits grain embargoes that withhold food from the hungry as a weapon against enemies, assures that food in reserves will benefit the very poor, requires the USA to negotiate with other grain-producing nations to establish emergency reserves that complement those of the USA, and establishes guidelines for working within developing nations to increase their food security.

In addition to legislative concerns, BREAD is aware that policies within an agency often have as much impact as the original legislation. In at least two areas, BREAD monitors closely the policies of the agencies: Agency for International Development, and to a lesser extent, the International Monetary Fund.

When deciding which legislation to push at a given time, BREAD uses practical political considerations of two types: first, proposals must have the backing and support of their own members, after careful education, and secondly, they promote those most in the public mind and most likely of success, consistent with long-term goals.

Many members of Congress work closely with Bread for the World; the most active are probably Senator Mark Hatfield, a member of the Board, and Congressman Paul Simons, a brother of the President. At this time, an aggressive effort is being made to enlist more Republicans into support of the philosophy and program of the organization.

In an interview with Barbara Howell and Loretta Hanson of the Washington office, they revealed that Bread for the World is beginning an emphasis on "Land and Hunger." The underlying issue is the need for reform of land ownership patterns.

In a Background Paper, Erik Eckholm presented this issue from the perspective of the Worldwatch Institute. After noting that the landless and near landless are usually the poorest people in a country, he stated, "Hundreds of millions of families are struggling to improve their lives through agriculture, but they lack secure access to the basis of agricultural life -- farmland." While land reform is widely recognized as a necessary ingredient in overcoming world hunger and poverty, "few goals have been so little implemented in practice."[14]

An Evaluation

Bread for the World is on course in setting as its goal the elimination of hunger and malnutrition on a global basis. It is committed to working at the level of public policy. Its membership is growing rapidly. There is a strong education program; materials are produced and sent monthly to members, providing them with information and perspective. The movement is organized by Congressional Districts, and people are trained to write and telegraph their Congressmen with specific requests. The staff is composed of highly dedicated and sacrificial Christian persons.

The legislative program is positive in that BREAD makes an annual decision as to its own agenda, rather than to react to legislation proposed by others.

However, a critical review raises some important questions:

1. BREAD appears to have backed away somewhat from dealing with large, systemic issues related to the international economy. BREAD had two staff members who were experts on the international economic order -- Terry Martin and Brenon Jones. Both were reported to have left because they were discouraged from devoting most of their time to these basic issues. Their replacements, Lane Vanderslice and Jim Edgerton, are working on grain reserves and related issues, but appear to be doing less than their predecessors on issues raised by the Group of 77.

2. The Board of Directors seems to increasingly favor issues that are easier for the grass-roots membership to understand and which can provide annual legislative victories as a way to provide the organization with a continuing series of successes. This sense of achievement is a necessary concern for a grass-roots organization. Most staff members appear to be aware of the necessary tension between the prophetic role and the requirement to understand and appreciate those who hold a different perspective. BREAD appears to be trying to challenge its members without alienating them.

3. There might be a closer amount of cooperation between BREAD and the Interreligious Task Force in setting legislative priorities and in working for passage of bills. At present, the two groups work together on some domestic issues, but their agendas differ on global concerns, and even where they overlap, there is little coordinated action.

4. The issue-selection process has focused on large issues at the philosophical level such as resolutions in the House and Senate in 1976 which support world food programs and enough for everyone to eat, and a general commitment to the Presidential Commission's Report, but in terms of legislation that has a price tag, this year the BREAD programs have relatively small dollar amounts and do not make the substantial contribution one would hope to the total elimination of poverty in the world. Passage of other aspects of their legislative agenda would make a substantial impact on world hunger.

5. There appears to be some lack of communication between the BREAD policy analysts located in New York and those in Washington, D.C., and between those in New York and the Interreligious Task Force, especially in the area of the international economic order.

6. BREAD has not concentrated its lobbying on those who make U.S. policy on United Nations issues as they relate to the basic structures of the world economy.

After offering criticisms of an outstanding organization, the impartial observer recognizes the substantial contribution made by BREAD to the effort to build a world without hunger.

VII. THE INTERRELIGIOUS TASK FORCE ON U.S. FOOD POLICY

The Interreligious Task Force on U. S. Food Policy (Taskforce) has 44 Washington-based staff members who are employed by national religious agencies. They work together to influence U.S. food policy and help the American religious community to do the same. The basic purpose of the Taskforce is "bread and justice for all." Twenty-eight Protestant, Roman Catholic, Jewish, and ecumenical agencies and networks cooperate in its work.

The Taskforce was organized following the World Food Conference in Rome in 1974. Church leaders met on December 16 and 17 at the Graymoor Unity Center in Garrison, New York to discuss how hunger-related public policy issues might be addressed ecumenically. Each denomination was in the process of establishing a special hunger-related program, and leaders felt that some funds should be made available for a joint public policy legislative emphasis. The organization was born in January 1975. The Reverend George Chauncey, who was the guiding influence in this organizing meeting, has served as Chair ever since.

The four committees of the Taskforce were determined by the initial agenda: (1) U.S. development and food assistance policy, (2) U.S. agricultural policy, (3) U.S. domestic nutrition programs, and (4) U.S. international economic policy. Across the years the emphasis has shifted from domestic issues to the global dimensions of hunger.

The Taskforce operating budget for FY 1980 was $196,000. Financial support comes from member denominations and organizations. The largest contributions for 1980 were:

> United Presbyterian Church.........$39,000
> United Methodist Church............37,700
> Presbyterian Church in the U.S......21,500
> Episcopal Church...................20,000
> United Church of Christ............12,000
> Lutheran Church in America..........7,000
> Christian Church (Disciples)........5,500
> American Baptists...................5,200
> American Lutheran Church............4,500

Each year elected representatives of the cooperating bodies meet to set priorities on areas for emphasis. Recommendations are prepared for the representatives by the Board of Directors and staff. The organization strives for consensus, so that one member can effectively block a proposed policy position, and indeed, this has happened on occasion.

A staff of seven or eight full-time persons works with the 44 part-time executives on loan from the denominations. The process used in developing policy positions is to document facts with care, test their interpretations with others, turn to experts for advice, use an elaborate process for building consensus, and seek to be consistent with the social pronouncements of the denominations. The Taskforce speaks in its own name and not on behalf of its constituents.

Research findings and policy positions are presented as one-issue statements in Hunger. The newsletter reaches some 13,000 persons each month through the IMPACT network. With copies distributed through denominational channels, the total circulation of each issue is about 35,000. In addition, Food Policy Notes go to about 600 key persons who work on hunger issues, the mailing list supplied by the denominations.

A Biblical and theological statement under the heading, "The Clarity of the Word of God" is unambiguous and powerful. The Taskforce proclaimed:

> The wretched of the earth are God's children,
> given irreducible dignity and worth by the endless
> love of God.... Precisely because these neighbors

are weak and hungry and poor and oppressed, they
have a special place in God's heart.... Because
God is for the poor, God is against exploitation
of the poor.... Our nation, like every other
nation, stands under God.... God's cause is the
cause of liberation and justice -- the cause of
feeding the hungry and liberating the oppressed
.... There is no way that any of us can be faithful
to the Lord of life without being faithful to this
cause.[15]

Recent Legislative Emphases

Tim Atwater is a full-time employee of the Taskforce who works in the
field of the international economic order. His work is directed by a Board
committee in this area. He is one of a rare group of persons who works for
the churches full-time in research and policy formulation in this field,
although others do so on a part-time basis.

The primary emphasis during July 1981 was preparation for the global
conference on North-South issues to be held in Mexico in October. The
Taskforce was also working on a bill to rescind the present requirement that
grain in the Food for Peace program must be shipped on vessels in the U.S.
maritime fleet. By not having to pay the exorbitant prices for use of these
vessels, Food for Peace would have $75 million more to use for purchase of
grain. Interestingly, Senator Jesse Helms of North Carolina led the floor
fight on its behalf. However, it appears that the bill has not received
sufficient support to pass this session of Congress.

The Infact Formula Issue has been in the forefront of attention, and
the Taskforce gave it priority consideration earlier in 1981. In that instance
it was considered good strategy to get a resolution passed in both Houses of
Congress supporting the position of the churches. On May 21, 1981 the World
Health Organization's 34th Assembly voted 118 to 1 to adopt a code of conduct
designed to restrict the promotion of infant formula. The United States
stood alone in voting against the code. Following that vote the House resolution in support of the WHO vote was passed by a majority of 301 to 100,
and in the Senate the vote was 89 to 2 against the Administration's position.
This helped to focus public attention on the issue even more. The Taskforce
has 1,600 newspaper articles from all parts of the nation on the WHO vote
and/or the Congressional resolutions. In a national poll, 50 percent of the
American people said they knew about the issue and 75 percent of them disagreed
with the Reagan Administration. The Taskforce felt it was equally important
to tell third world countries that the sentiments of Congress and the American
people were different from the official position.

During the first half of 1980 the Taskforce gave attention to lobbying
the Congress in order to get the IMF to consider basic human needs in formu-
lating economic stabilization policies. This work was a continuation of an
emphasis from the previous year. Just before a vote in the Congress on
September 17, 1980 on HR 7244, a bill to authorize U.S. participation in the

Seventh Quota Increase for the International Monetary Fund in the amount of $5.5 billion, George Chauncey wrote to all members of Congress:

> We recommend that you vote against HR 7244 unless
> it is amended to include language which would
> provide greater attention to the impact of IMF
> policies on the ability of poor people in developing
> countries to meet their basic human needs. There is
> need for an effective international institution
> able to provide national governments with sound,
> impartial economic advice and assistance in address-
> ing balance of payment difficulties. Whether or not
> the IMF can be so reformed as to fulfill that need is,
> in our judgment, still an unanswered question.

In the October 17, 1980 Food Policy Notes the announcement was made:

> In recent days a major legislative victory has
> been won, with both the House and Senate agreeing
> on an amendment committing the U.S. to work
> actively for reforms in the IMF....President
> Carter signed the legislation.

The Law of the Sea Bill is expected to take a great deal of time and work next year; the United Methodists are taking the lead with their "Save the Seas" program.

An Evaluation

When denominational leaders were asked which organization is most effective in dealing with systemic causes underlying world hunger, most of them gave first place to this group.

Five strengths seem to distinguish the Taskforce. First is the leadership. The Reverend George Chauncey has the ability to express the profound nature of the Christian faith and the structural issues involved in overcoming malnutrition and hunger. His testimony on behalf of the churches before Congressional Committees is reported in superlative terms. His leadership style is collegial, so that he coordinates rather than controls and gives persons on the staff the feeling of importance in their own work.

Secondly, the staff is of sufficient size and commitment to do the research that is required for thorough social analysis. The 50 or more denominational leaders, staff, and interns do research, prepare the constant stream of literature, send it through their networks, and prepare materials for the lobbying that takes place on Capitol Hill.

Third, the materials are well written, dispassionate and morally rigorous. They take into account the feelings of those on the opposite side of issues, yet are always clear as to the views of the Taskforce. Part of this clarity comes from long discussions that precede policy decisions in the effort to build full consensus.

Fourth, the Taskforce has earned the respect of the Congress. Whether Congressmen agree or disagree with the policy position presented by a representative of the churches, they know that the concern for the poor is real, that the homework has been done thoroughly, and that the proposals are reasonable.

Finally, there is the capacity to distribute the findings to denominational leaders and to a network of people across the country. This is done directly through IMPACT and indirectly through the denominational literature of the 26 religous bodies represented on the Taskforce.

After recognizing the positive work done by the Taskforce, there are constructive criticisms and suggestions:

1. <u>Identifying a Food Policy Statement for the 1980's.</u> This important document presents three perspectives on root causes of world poverty; one factor is identified in each as the key problem. They are insufficient economic growth, dependency, and elitism. The Taskforce points to the truth in each perspective; without some economic growth the only thing to be distributed is poverty. The second analysis rightly calls attention to the wider context in which dependency has developed, while the third "provides an essential clue to the global development scene."[16]

The second analysis titled "dependency" does not even mention the words "justice" or "equity" of the global economic structures, but only the relationship of dependency. It does not challenge the United States as the chief actor in this drama to modify its own power positions to accommodate the needs of others. It fails to point out that from this central system of gross inequity flows the inevitability of poverty for others.

The total impression from the presentation is that the third area -- elitism -- which was presented last is the most important. The major concern is with how benefits from structural changes will be distributed within nations. The most space and attention is given to this analysis. While the fact of the global system is recognized, the shift of emphasis is disturbing.

2. <u>The health of the international community is not discussed.</u> The health of the world economy as a whole, more than any other factor, determines the fate of hundreds of millions of hungry people. Expanding trade, reducing inflation and stabilizing currency are some of the key elements in this healthy world economy. Everything the United States does, even in domestic policy, affects the health of the world economy. So large and important a group as the Taskforce, it would seem, should watch and report on the implications of American economic policy on the world economy.

3. <u>Identity with the Group of 77.</u> While the Taskforce has studied the meetings of the United Nations in which the Group of 77 has sought to move toward a new international economic order and has had a positive influence, the attitude of the Taskforce is disturbing. It has taken the approach that both the positions of the Group of 77 and the U.S. have been wrong at many points and, therefore, the Taskforce should stay at arm's

length from both sides while trying to structure the dialogue to support
the legitimate needs of the South. The approach gives the appearance of
objectivity, and certainly the churches would not want to identify with
every position of the South. But to stand with the poor nations in the
struggle is to buy into justice.

4. Too oriented toward Capitol Hill. Church-related groups need to
go beyond this center of power to the agencies that interpret and administer
policy, and to those who make and interpret policy of the United States in
the context of the United Nations. Since there is so much discretion in the
way policy is formulated and administered, this becomes as important as the
legislation itself. The Taskforce feels that it does not have the staff to
adequately cover the Hill, much less go beyond it. However, that assumption
needs to be questioned.

5. A greater ministry of envisioning. A weak point in the Taskforce
work appears to this writer to be a lack of imagination. Creative work is
done as small additions to bills or in the deletion of a section, rather than
in envisioning a larger program. Since there is so little time for people
in government to do creative thinking, this task is especially important for
the churches. A realistic vision of a legislative program for this nation
and the United Nations would at least provide direction and inspiration to
the churches.

6. The need to coordinate better with Bread for the World. Ms.
Janet Vandevender, Executive Director of the staff, stated in an interview
that the two hunger-related organizations are working together more closely
now than three or four years ago. The Taskforce realizes that BREAD has a
Board that is responsive to grass-roots outlooks, while the Taskforce has
to satisfy the interests of denominational representatives. However, the
impression at the Taskforce is that it is more broadguage and can work at
systemic levels more readily that BREAD's board will permit. There is truth
in this contention, but it seems to this writer that BREAD has a larger
vision than the Taskforce gives them credit for holding.

Tim Atwater and the Committee on International Economics in theory
support the proposal of BREAD that 50 percent of World Bank funds should be
used in programs that benefit the poor directly, but this has not become a
policy priority of the Taskforce, and no plans have been made to lobby for
the proposal.

In summary, the Taskforce is the best mechanism the churches have for
expressing their concerns on hunger policy. It is often an influential voice
in the halls of Congress. Its positions are clearcut and forceful. Not the
least of its strengths is the ability to educate denominational leaders.
However, because much has been given to the Taskforce, of it much is required.
The criticisms expressed should be understood in that light.

VIII. CHURCH WORLD SERVICE

Church World Service (CWS) was established in 1946 by 17 U.S. Protestant denominations to do post-war relief and rehabilitation work. CWS joined

the National Council of Churches of Christ in the USA (NCCC) in 1950 and the Council's Division of Overseas Ministries in 1964, where it became the development, relief and refugee assistance agency of the NCCC. As a unit of the Division of Overseas Ministries, CWS conforms to all NCCC policy statements and organizational plans.

Today CWS is the ecumenical expression of 31 Protestant and Orthodox churches representing over 40 million members in the USA. CWS cooperates with these churches and is their agent as they set the policies and provide the financial support for its ministry.

CWS works in more than 70 countries on five continents in the areas of development assistance, disaster response, assistance to refugees and displaced persons, and in the U.S. on constituency education and public policy advocacy. In all of its overseas work, CWS acts in ecumenical partnership with indigenous churches and church agencies. Activities are undertaken by local institutions, usually church-related, to which CWS channels funds, materials and personnel. These "colleague agencies" may have a traditional mission relationship with American churches; often funds go to strengthen the ability of these colleague agencies to operate more autonomously.

In addition, CWS relates to regional conferences of churches and national Christian councils. CWS also participates actively in the World Council of Churches' Commission on Inter-Church Aid, Refugees and World Service (CICARWS). CICARWS covers areas of the world where CWS does not have normal contact, but where a clear need has been identified.

The CWS mandate to meet human need sometimes leads to overseas cooperative programs with secular organizations, governments, quasi-governmental agencies and international organizations. CWS decides on a case-by-case basis whether to support particular projects. The decision is based on a number of factors including the priority of the problems being addressed, the receiving agency's commitment to the poor and oppressed, its reflective and decision-making capacities, its management and technical skills, its reporting procedures, and its willingness to cooperate with others when necessary.

CWS focuses on projects that help people become more self-reliant, that serve the poorest segments of society, that develop processes of community interaction, and that contribute to structural changes in unjust systems. The World Council emphasis on justice, participation and sustainability are used as criteria for evaluating these projects.

CWS's concern for justice leads to the commitment to impact directly on those living at subsistence levels with the aim of empowering the marginalized, in contrast to "trickle-down" approaches to development. It also addresses root causes of poverty within countries -- the concentration and exploitation of economic, social and political power.[17]

The 1980 Annual Report

The 1980 Annual Report provides a description of the work of the past year. A "Development Office" seeks to stay in touch with other agencies and organizations in the field of development and is beginning a computerized library in order to gain immediate access to what is happening in the field. The office also supplies prospective donors with an annual "Project List" along with the cost.

The "Emergency and Disaster Response" Office reported fifteen appeals for disaster relief in Asia, Africa, Europe, Latin American and the Caribbean in 1980. The size and intensity of human-caused disasters seem to be increasing. By far the largest area of work was with refugees from Viet Nam. The two major disasters that are increasing in scope are Somalia and the Afghans fleeing to Pakistan. The work is divided into three phases: (1) immediate aid in the form of clothing, blankets, shelter, medicine and food; (2) rehabilitation and reconstruction; and (3) long-term improvements and pre-disaster planning.

Financial support for CWS in 1980 was $61,247,000. It came from:

```
Support Program, U.S. Government .......$19,248,000 or 31.4%
Member Denominations....................13,419,000 or 21.9
Contributed Commodities.................13,033,000 or 21.3
CWS/CROP  Hunger and Clothing Appeals.....9,506,000 or 14.5
Miscellaneous...........................7,100,000 or 11.1
```

The U.S. Government contribution was larger than usual, but nearly all of the increase was used for service to refugees. CWS also received federal Food for Peace commodities which were used in five country programs.

It is instructive to note that .2% of the funds of CWS were spent in the United States for education about development needs, the causes of poverty, and for public policy advocacy. In the annual report of 37 pages, three paragraphs were devoted to the Office on Development Policy where Larry Minear and Carol Capps are representatives for Development Policy. The first paragraph described the participation of the office in passing a bill in Congress late in 1980, a U.S. food security reserve of four million tons of wheat. The second paragraph mentioned the fact of monitoring a range of international basic human-needs issues without naming them, and stated the CWS participation in the work of the Interreligious Task Force on U.S. Food Policy. The final paragraph stated that the Washington staff represented CWS at the Eleventh Special Session of the UN on North-South cooperation and served on the U.S. delegation to the UN Food Council meeting in Tanzania.

Other Publications

Three publications were reviewed over a period of two years to see how much the root causes of hunger were discussed. First, World Hunger describes itself as a "continuing report on present conditions and what the churches are doing about them..." The second is CWS Update, and the third is Service News. There is little about systemic causes underlying hunger in the first two of these publications, with some more in the latter. The May 1981 Service News contains an urgent appeal to write to Congress on the Infant Formula issue. The August/September 1980 issue contains a major section as a report on the Presidential Commission on World Hunger. An article on "Global Economics and Hunger" reported on the book Hunger for Justice by Jack A. Nelson. There was also an excellent bibliography on Global Economics and hunger. In September 1979, an article "Multinationals: Friend or Foe?" gave a presentation of good and bad aspects of multinationals.

A Working Paper Titled "Areas of Consideration"

In a top-level working paper titled "Areas of Consideration" the staff of CWS was invited to discuss proposed projects and issues before they are adopted officially. When revised and accepted they will become the guide for action during the next three years. The considerations of a substantive nature are in six categories: (1) development, (2) organization support for self-reliance, (3) assistance to refugees and displaced persons, (4) emergencies and disasters, (5) global education and public policy advocacy, and (6) resource management. For the purposes of this study only the fifth area will be discussed.

The document begins with "the problem." It states that because of its economic resources and political power the United States has a leading role in shaping global conditions. However, too often U.S. policy is based on short-term interest. Special interest groups such as U.S.-based multinational corporations, farm organizations, consumers, labor groups and domestic manufacturers, constantly address international trade issues in terms that benefit them, but there is no readily identifiable constituency which reviews U.S. policies from a global humanitarian perspective.

> The influence of those who would use U.S. policies
> for narrow gain needs to be offset by supporters of
> just, compassionate and responsible U.S. policies.[18]

The "Response" of CWS is to complement its support of overseas activities with education for global justice and public policy advocacy in the U.S. These functions are designed to support its "primary responsibilities" of development, relief and refugee assistance.

In the area of global education, CWS states its commitment to having the voice of the poor and oppressed help shape programs and evaluate success and failure. CWS also recognizes that an educational effort is necessary in the United States to help citizens understand conditions of world hunger and its causes. Hence CWS works in global education to complement denominational and other efforts.

In the area of Public Policy Advocacy there is only one paragraph. Advocacy allows CWS to interpret its perspective to those who determine U.S. government policy. The four areas in which U.S. policy is to be assessed are (1) addressing the root causes of poverty in the developing nations; (2) responding to basic human needs without allowing political considerations to outweigh the need to save and promote human life; (3) providing assistance commensurate with the economic resources available to the U.S.; and (4) appropriately regulating activities of U.S. corporations doing business in the third world.

The Office of Public Policy

As noted in the section on the Lutheran Churches, the salaries of Larry Minear and Carol Capps in the Washington office are paid at the level of 60 percent by Church World Service and 40 percent by Lutheran World Relief.

Larry Minear is Secretary of the Interreligious Task Force, a member of the Administrative Committee, and as such has a final review on letters to Congress, publications and policy decisions.

Carol Capps is a member of the Board of the Task Force and Chair of the International Development Assistance workgroup. She has been especially active in lobbying to get restored an appropriation of $500,000 for the UN Voluntary Fund for the Decade for Women which supports small-scale development efforts that help women. Because of an anti-Israeli resolution passed in Copenhagen at the Conference on Women in Development, some Jewish groups in the United States have succeeded in eliminating the money in the House bill. A major effort through coalition building and education is being mounted to have it restored.

CROP

To complete the account it is necessary to review the work of CROP. Originally known as the Christian Rural Overseas Program, CROP began in 1947 as an arm of CWS. Its purpose was to gather wheat and other crops from American farmers for shipment to Europe. In 1966 the name was changed to CROP (no longer an acronym) and urban campaigns were initiated along with those of rural areas. CROP is the hunger education and fund-raising arm of CWS. With headquarters in Elkhart, Indiana, CWS/CROP has field offices in 25 locations, especially in the midwest and north central farm regions of the nation.

A discussion with the Director of the CROP office in Columbia, Maryland confirmed reports from others about the way these offices are operated. The Director, who was cooperative and enthusiastic, told how she combines presenting the story of hunger with fund-raising appeals. She prefers not to get into issues of social justice "because they do not help the fund-raising." Her approach is to build a simple, direct identification with the hungry of the world and ask for a response of compassion and sharing. She is, however, willing to discuss systemic issues when requested to do so.

CROP Constituency Education Pilot Program

In September 1974 the CROP National Committee decided to sponsor a Development Education Program. To its primary mandate, "to conduct appeals for materials and funds" was added a second: "CROP, also, through these campaigns and related means, informs and sensitizes American people in support of self-development of people around the world." This purpose was conceived as having three parts: education into the day-to-day problems of existence of people in the third world, into policies and actions in the developed world which tend to perpetuate these problems, and actions which can be taken by U.S. citizens to help overcome these problems.

There was considerable doubt within CROP about the wisdom of this program, and some opposed it. Earlier, in March of 1974, the CROP Director had reported to staff that some feared fund-raising might be neglected and that getting into political education would alienate some supporters and thus reduce contributions.

The program emerged slowly. Little was heard about it publicly until a year later when Paul McCleary, CWS Executive Director, at a national Executive Committee Meeting, identified one of CROP's strengths as "education on development" and the "mobilization of persons around hunger-related issues." At this meeting on October 16, 1975 the project plans began to be formulated.

On February 12, 1976 there was a first staff consultation on Development Education. The purposes were set forth: (1) to hold justice as the constant criterion and ultimate goal for development; (2) to illuminate the root causes of hunger, poverty, underdevelopment and injustice; (3) to enable persons to participate in development; (4) to use the world food crisis as a focal point for a broad range of concerns; and (5) to identify a specific and appropriate role for CROP rather than try to do everything.

A year later, on September 27, 1977, Daniel L. Force was employed to begin the project. Along with his wife, Loretta Walen Force, who wrote the final report of the Pilot Program, he did research for a year, designed a conceptual framework for development education, and then conducted pilot projects in several midwestern communities.

The report, dated November 1979, is one of the finest documents available on the rationale for a global approach to issues of hunger and poverty. It offers a pedogogical framework as to how people can learn about others in distant parts of the world and then develop a willingness to become involved in the struggle for justice for those far away. An important section of the report describes how churches in other nations devote considerable time and money to development education. For example, in the United Kingdom, Christian Aid, which is the equivalent to Church World Service, spends five percent of its annual income on educating the church constituency. There are staff ministers to church-related youth groups, to schools of theology, to colleges and universities, and to primary and secondary schools. These persons design written materials for each constituency and constantly go speak in the cause of development education. The field staff assists 2,500 Christian Aid committees throughout the United Kingdom to do both fund-raising and education.

The churches of Canada have a large annual development education program, "Ten Days for World Development." It is a joint program of Canada's mainline churches -- Anglican, Catholic, Lutheran, Presbyterian and United Churches of Canada. Their effort has been supported by a subsidy from the Canadian International Development Agency. Its concerns are derived from Biblical and Christian social justice traditions which favor the poor, the oppressed and the powerless of society.

"Ten Days" has a deliberate international and third world focus that reminds Canadians of the needs and aspirations of the vast majority of their fellow human beings in the South; at the same time consideration is given to changes needed in Canadian society that are required to benefit third world peoples. While this is a ten-day emphasis throughout the nation once a year, the thrust behind it is political education on a year-long basis. The program operates in 50 communities. It does not raise funds, but the ten days are during Lent and churches raise funds for global concerns during this time. Finally, the staff is working to build development education into traditional education programs of the churches.

The report notes how the World Council of Churches at Montreux in 1970 recommended that development funds of the churches should be used for two types of action of equal importance: financing of development projects, and education programs to mobilize public opinion and to finance political action, "especially in the affluent countries, to foster world cooperation for development."

In line with the tone of optimism then prevailing, it was felt that up to 25 percent of available resources should be spent on educational programs. The purpose was "to sustain the intellectual and spiritual thrust until the desired attitudinal and structural changes occur in the developed world, as well as in those developing countries where existing structures impede or repress development."

No such large amounts were ever spent on development education. CROP's constituency education staff concluded, "By and large it was too difficult for the churches to mount campaigns which basically would have put into question the existing order of western capitalist societies."[19]

The Constituency Education Pilot Program Director feels the reform of public education from the elementary level through the university is as basic as providing better materials for Christian education. Barely five percent of teachers preparing for positions from kindergarten through twelfth grade levels have any exposure at all to international studies in their training; American students come out next to last on international surveys about international institutions and processes; and only three percent of all undergraduate students enroll in any courses dealing particularly with world affairs.[20]

An Evaluation

CWS provides a splendid example of ecumenical cooperation among denominations and other organizations. It is sensitive to indigenous churches and organizations in the third world and works through them in its development projects. CWS has worked with governments and other secular groups but has been careful to maintain its own integrity in the process.

In all the CWS and CROP literature there is an emphasis on a movement from relief and rehabilitation into development projects which purport to address underlying causes of hunger and poverty. However, when the 1980 budget is examined, only 10 percent or $6 million of a total expenditure of slightly more than $60 million is spent on development.

The reasons given as underlying causes of world hunger and poverty are of secondary importance in the view of this writer. Very little was found in the literature that gets to the heart of the matter. Almost nothing is written on the international economic order or the U.S. pattern of consistently thwarting the rest of the world in working toward new arrangements that are more just. Staff members insist that Dr. Paul F. McCleary, Executive Director, speaks out on systemic issues at every possible opportunity, but there appears to be considerable resistance to a strong emphasis by other staff and some constituent denominations, who fear it will subtract from the enthusiasm for fund-raising and relief/development projects.

The CROP offices combine fund-raising and hunger education and provide substantial support to the total income of CWS. However, one must raise the question as to whether constituency education is seen as a promotional tool to raise more money, or as a way of helping people understand the real issues in world hunger and U.S. complicity in them.

The CROP Global Education Pilot Project is substantively different from regular CROP education. This project is outstanding in its conceptual framework, pedogogy, and depth of understanding. Indeed, the report of the Pilot Years is one of the best documents available on development education. The CWS is well advised to begin spending significant amounts of money and energy in educating its constituents within the framework of this model.

The funds expended for Global Education and public policy advocacy in the United States amount to only two-tenths of one percent of total funds expended, a far cry from the five percent spent in Great Britain, or the 25 percent recommended by the World Council of Churches in 1970. Moreover, this observer got the impression from public literature and the long-range planning document that those in control wish to pass over this work as quickly as possible. This small expenditure reflects an attitude that does not seem to take seriously the expressed need to build support for a compassionate and responsible U.S. public policy to offset the power of special interest groups. Poor David does not even have a slingshot to use against the Goliath of this battle!

One must conclude that the quality of the material presented to the public and the amount expended on public policy advocacy are grossly inadequate when judged in the light of the size and scope of this organization.

IX. INSTITUTE FOR FOOD AND DEVELOPMENT POLICY

Louis L. Knowles, who directs the Coordinating Council for Hunger Concerns for the National Council of Churches, stated in an interview in June 1981 that in his judgment the writings of Frances Moore Lappe and William Valentine and the work of their Institute for Food and Development Policy are becoming increasingly influential in shaping the policies and thinking of the churches in the area of world hunger.

Their early book, Food First, Beyond the Myth of Scarcity, has been read widely. A new study guide was published in 1980 titled What Can We Do? It was funded by Oxfam-America and the United Methodist Church. General financial support for the Institute is received from a number of private foundations, and from the Church of the Brethern, Episcopal Church, Maryknoll Fathers, and the United Presbyterian Church.

The materials published by this Institute have a very carefully thought-out perspective. The way to evaluate any development program, they believe, is to ask how it contributes to the goal of an equitable sharing of power. Such a criterion keeps us from the pitfall of assuming that greater production equals development, if more people suffer because of it. They conclude that, based on this criterion, the U.S. AID program, on balance, has done more harm than good.

The next step in their analysis is to identify the factors in an economic system that generate inequitable concentrations of power. They decry the "free market" concept because those with greater wealth can maximize gains and get greater control. Once this concentration of power is under way, it is self-reinforcing. Those with economic and political power can direct policy decisions to favor themselves. For our society, or any other, they feel, the question is not whether there will be planning, but rather whether the planning will be done democratically and, therefore, take into account the needs of all.

> Our vision, then, is...equitable sharing in control
> over production resources and democratic planning
> in which all people's needs are taken into account.

Valentine and Lappe concentrate on empowering the poor within societies. They urge development of small-scale alternative economic and social structures in which there is more equitable sharing of economic power.

In their major book and in the newer study guide there is no hint that their principles might apply to the one basic structure -- the international political economy. But the principles of greater democracy in the planning process and more equitable sharing in control over production resources can also be applied to the relationship among nations, as well as to institutions within nations.

This analysis provides another perspective from which to challenge the Churches. Obviously, a great deal can be said for support of small-scale development that begins to empower the poor. One need not quarrel with the analysis and the work of the Institute in terms of what they are doing. But one must object strenuously to what they are not doing. They imply that they are providing the churches and the public with a basic approach to the problems related to world hunger and poverty. But while the kinds of projects they support can be useful in small ways, the fact remains tha they are not dealing with the central issues. Indeed, they appear to be directing attention away from the rigorous analysis and critical action that is needed to change the global systemic patterns underlying world hunger and poverty.[21]

CHAPTER FOUR

AN EVALUATION OF THE CHURCHES' RESPONSE -- WITH SUGGESTIONS

I. THREE APPROACHES TO EVALUATION

In evaluating church-related programs one always brings a theoretical model of the underlying causes of hunger to the analysis. What the churches propose as the solution depends in large part on their understanding of the cause. One type of evaluation begins by reviewing the development models held by those who operate church programs.

An evaluation can also be made of the whole range of things the churches are actually doing -- from programs of relief, rehabilitation and development, to educating their members, to the extent and quality of lobbying efforts backed by grass-roots movements.

Finally, one can approach the question of how to deal with world hunger from the perspective used by the World Council of Churches. The churches can look at the international economic order as well as that within each nation and ask three questions: Is it just? Is it participatory? Is it sustainable?

The criteria set forth here can be used by church leaders in evaluating their own programs. Let us turn briefly to consider each of these perspectives.

Four Theoretical Models of the World Community[1]

(a) Underdevelopment as backwardness

The basic question is how to bring backward nations into the twentieth century. The problem is "out there" and so the solution is "out there." The strategy is to provide educational opportunity, modernization, scientific thought, and modern management. The appeal is to charity in the framework of the donor-receiver. Christian appeals are to compassion, mercy, and love of neighbor.

(b) Underdevelopment as "dependent development"

The basic assumption here is that nations are poor and people are hungry because they have accepted a dependent relationship that must be broken. The strategy proposed is self-reliant development and disassociation

99

from centers of power. The pedagogical approach is to experience liberation and learn from that experience. Christians of the North are asked to express solidarity with the poor of the South but to stand back and let them organize their own liberation. Church-related assistance should be small-scale projects that provide opportunities for liberation and new appropriate technologies that free without being disruptive to indiginous cultural patterns. Christians of the North are challenged to change their life-styles toward more simplicity and more conscientious use of scarce resources.

(c) Underdevelopment as injustice
within developing countries

The problem is elite minorities within developing nations who control ownership of land, means of production and access to educational opportunity. These elites make the agreements with international banks and development assistance programs of individual nations in such a manner that projects are used to confirm and strengthen themselves at the expense of the masses. The proposal is to lessen military assistance to dictators who serve these elites, insist on human rights, encourage land reform and target all development assistance into projects that directly benefit the poorest segments of each society. The strategy is to cut back assistance to countries with greater inequity or repression and to reward countries that seek to serve the needs of their poorest members. The basic concept is justice and equity "out there" with the implicit belief that there is little to be gained by working for justice in the international order if injustice is to be the rule within national orders.

(d) Underdevelopment as unjust
global economic relations

The historical framework for this perspective is the colonial system. The "have" nations of the North systematically conquered, ruled, and used the "have not" nations of the South for more than 200 years, with most of these colonies gaining their independence only since World War II. Patterns of trade, pricing structures, and opportunity to control the use of commodities by manufacturing them into finished products, for example, are largely the decisions of the stronger industrialized nations and are made to benefit those in power. The strategy proposed for dealing with this imbalance is the New International Economic Order. The pedagogical approach for educating the church members is based on understanding these relationships between rich and poor nations as both being part of a single system. The basic concepts are justice, enlightened self-interest, and the necessity of working together in an interdependent world that is rapidly becoming a single global community.

There is truth in each of these positions, and any one that is used exclusively without taking into account the truth in the others will be partial and inadequate. However, the special concern of this study is with the fourth position. Nations of the South do need educational opportunities and modernization, and there is an intense desire for these opportunities throughout the South. They will come with startling rapidity as money becomes available for this purpose. The danger for nations of the South is that they will simply copy their richer brothers of the North, rather than take what is useful and integrate it into their own cultures, value systems and religious orientations.

While nations and the people within them yearn to become free from dependent relationships, the end is not independence but rather interdependence. Liberation economically as well as politically is a process that goes on even while interdependent relationships are being formed. It is unrealistic now for most nations to withdraw into independence, although China did it rather successfully for almost 30 years. But in the single body of a world community the parts cannot function in isolation. It is usually irresponsible to become a dropout, even though dropouts sometimes make positive contributions. Blocks of countries can align to take strong positions in the interest of justice, and alternative social and political organizations and lifestyles can be explored in an effort to support liberation. Indeed, within our interdependent global community we will express our humanity best by striving to make the world safe for diversity.

Likewise, the third set of assumptions on injustice within nations is valid but, as has been stated elsewhere, does not constitute an argument for ignoring the central global patterns. The writer was a minister in the southern United States during the racial revolution in the 1950s and 1960s and remembers well the argument that to give blacks better wages, opportunities to purchase homes, and other economic benefits would be wasted. The assumption was that if blacks got money they would either destroy themselves through excessive drinking or they would buy big cars. In neither case would any useful purpose be served. While some whites had observed this behavior in some blacks, it was nonetheless an improper generalized assumption, and it did not seem to predict what would happen in the future when sustained wealth and opportunity were within the reach of a large number of black citizens. By analogy, it is probable that in many countries economic reforms will come as wealth expands and opportunities become more available. Generally, this will happen as nations have opportunity over time to participate more equitably in the international economic order. Church leaders are in danger of falling into a subtle paternalism by saying if poor nations get more income it will only go to the wealthy or to corrupt leaders. A stereotype of mismanagement by elites of the third world can be used by opponents of development to justify their obstructionist tactics.

What Churches Are Actually Doing

A second approach to evaluation is to ask what the churches are actually doing about hunger in the world. This can be done at many levels:

Amount and Quality of Relief, Rehabilitation, and Development Projects

Most denominations have direct service programs in each of these areas, although the United Presbyterian USA has chosen to work instead through interdenominational agencies. The amount of money raised and the extent of the programs in each of these areas is significant. Most denominations, as well as the Church World Service are turning much of their public relations focus toward development, yet most of their money is still spent on relief. The scope of this study did not permit the evaluation of the effectiveness of these programs, except in general terms. One can ask how cooperative each group is with others in overall planning, how much each spends, how well each group reaches and serves the poorest people, and how creative each is in designing projects for development which grow toward self-help and are sustainable.

The Presidential Commission on World Hunger concluded that churches and other private groups are far more effective in their role as development agencies than in their relief efforts.[2]

(b) Public Policy Statements

Every denomination or hunger organization has public literature which sets forth the basic assumptions on which its program is built. Most denominations have official statements which serve as the rationale for programs, and most try to deal with systemic causes underlying world hunger. A review of this literature provides mixed results; seldom are statements incorrect. The problem is one of highlighting minor points and failing to deal fully with the major realities. Also, one must be aware that organizations do not always practice what they claim to believe.

(c) Education Programs

Some denominations have organizations at the parish level that are active in hunger issues. Most have study books on hunger-related issues which have been used voluntarily by parishes thoroughout the denominations. Many have specialists at the national level who go to local parishes or to district meetings and conferences and teach courses on world hunger. However, many of these courses, in an effort to begin where people live, are so tied to the immediate concerns of the participants that there is little time to deal with the broad and basic systemic causes that underlie world hunger. If one gets into these issues, time is needed to do so in some depth — a little learning in this field does not change lifelong attitudes. There are those with wealth and power, like Zaccheus, who climb their sycamore tree to see Jesus. A confused or apologetic presentation will not lead them to announce that they have decided to divide their wealth with those they have wronged. Again, most of the churches' written materials lack depth and comprehension adequate for dealing with the realities that must be faced.

(d) Lobbying

Most of the denominational lobbying is coordinated through the Interreligious Task Force on U.S. Food Policy, with Bread for the World being the other lobbying organization that is most effective. This lobbying effort has made significant impact at certain key points. One cannot expect more from the lobby than can be delivered by the constituency that backs those who speak before Congressional committees and in the cloak rooms of the House and Senate. Basic questions to ask about lobbying activities are: How insightful is the group in choosing issues that really make a difference and at the same time have the possibility for passage? Does the organization go beyond law making in Congress and seek to influence agency policy? Does the organization lobby through the State Department, the Treasury Department and other agencies concerned with United Nations policies and those of the world banking organizations?

(e) Quality of Leadership Elites

Churches and organizations they spawn that deal with world hunger issues are no more effective than the quality of their leadership. How much understanding and courage do these organizational leaders display? Do they hold a strong vision of a world without hunger to which constituents can respond? Are they creative in their vision and positive in their actions?

The World Council of Churches

The World Council of Churches has provided helpful criteria for evaluating any program for action sponsored by the churches. They ask three simple but profound questions: Is it just? Is it participatory? Is it sustainable?

(a) Is It Just?

Some denominations pass beautifully worded resolutions at national conventions about the importance of justice, but do not relate the general ideal to specific problems of the global community or to injustices within nations. In the long term, the solution to the problem of hunger on a global scale is the power of justice to work in the minds and hearts of people. Christians believe that God can sensitize the human conscience so that those who perpetuate injustice become willing to have the patterns of power changed. This process of change is never easy but it is always possible. The churches have a unique role to play in their proclamation of justice as the will of God and as the basis for all humane society. Every program can be evaluated on the basis of how well the churches hold up the ideal of justice and how much they work to see it realized.

(b) Is It Participatory?

The strategy of the churches should always be to work toward maximum participation and fair representation of all nations in the global social contract, and then to empower all groups within societies to make effective demands of their social systems.

Justice and participation go hand in hand. Those who do not have the opportunity to participate will usually become victims of injustice. The churches need to ask whether the policies of multinational corporations within countries or the aid programs of the United States lead to wider participation, or whether they strengthen elites who in turn use their power to become more entrenched in favored positions. The development programs sponsored by the churches have a good record in enabling recipients to participate actively.

(c) Is It Sustainable?

Some issues that are raised by the question have to do with environmental impact. Do farming practices erode the soil? Are the oceans depleted by overfishing? Other issues relate to use of irreplaceable and finite natural resources. Can we sustain the profligate use of oil when the world's supply is being exhausted rapidly? Other concerns deal with political power. Can the United States continue to act independently and arbitrarily in a world that is dangerously near annihilation because of advanced missiles and bombs? Can the United States assume that its power is unlimited in a world that has become interdependent? Would it not be wiser to build long-term systems for world order with regular channels for redress of grievance?

Denominational leaders and representative lay persons may find it profitable to come together for purposes of review and evaluation of hunger programs based on these criteria or others they might design.

II. A MORE PROPHETIC ROLE FOR THE CHURCHES

The Old Testament prophets had the genius of keen social analysis. They saw the root causes of poverty as injustice and oppression and they spoke for a God who despised their worship or offerings until they dealt with the injustice within their society.

One in four persons on planet earth has a total annual income in U.S. dollars at the 1976 level of $200 per year or less. Almost one in five persons, or 500 million, is malnourished and hungry. At the same time, the wealthy of the North are growing richer, so that the gap between rich and poor continues to widen. The United States, with its six percent of the world's population, consumes a ton of grain annually for each person; the average in the South is less than 500 pounds. This same six percent uses almost 40 percent of scarce energy resources of the globe.

Justice or Charity?

What attitude shall the churches take toward these poor countries and peoples? Do we assume a special right to our favored status and great wealth? When we are generous is it in the form of charity for the starving, or is it an effort to restructure the economic order so as to provide a more equitable distribution of earth's resources, even when we are the favored few?

Irving Kristol, in midyear 1975, was disturbed by the lack of gratitude of the third world countries. He expressed the ethic of charity and rejected the ethic of justice when he wrote:

> There is always a good case, in both principle and
> prudence, for the more affluent being charitable
> toward the poor -- even to those whose poverty is

largely their own fault. Nor is there any reason
to expect, much less insist on gratitude; such
benevolence is supposed to be its own reward.
But when the poor start 'mau-mauing' their
actual or potential benefactors, when they
begin vilifying them, insulting them, demanding
as of right what is not theirs to demand --
then one's sense of self-respect may properly
take precedence over one's self-imposed
humanitarian obligations.[3]

Parallel Movements: American Civil Rights and the Struggle of the Group of 77

Some of the finest hours in American church history came during the
time of involvement in the American civil rights struggle. Black churches
led and many white churches joined, creating a movement that changed public
perception to the point where civil rights legislation could be passed. The
result was a change in the structures of our society so that blacks had
better opportunity for jobs, equal pay for equal work, and the ability to
move from ghettos into formerly all-white neighborhoods. In general, a new
day of opportunity dawned as justice was established in the social order.

This movement began slowly and was extremely costly to many persons,
including a host of ministers who lost their pastorates. Church contributions
were cut at times because irate members did not agree with the drive for
economic and social justice. While Martin Luther King, Jr. gave it tremendous
impetus, in another sense he was the product of this widespread movement
that was in progress.

The Group of 77 comes to the General Assembly of the United Nations
and pleads for elementary steps toward establishing justice in the social
order. The American government has stood, as did Governor Wallace at the
door of the University of Alabama to keep black students out, as the chief
antagonist of these poor nations, often refusing to hear their positions, and
when compelled to do so, procrastinating and offering crumbs rather than
bread. Finally, in time, concessions are made as further pressure is applied,
much in the way they were made to blacks in the South as a result of sit-
ins, sermons, economic boycotts and other forms of pressure. One role of the
American church now is that which was assumed by white Christians in the civil
rights movement. It was clear to those who were favored that they must
stand alongside the victims of injustice.

The movement that is needed is hard to organize. It is difficult to
spark the imagination of Americans because poor countries are far removed
from their lives and because very few Americans have even an elementary understanding of the issues. The average American does not perceive the injustice
as being real, hence she/he is not prone to consider changing these structures.
And yet, the world is rapidly increasing in interdependence so that we are now
a single system. In this community, most of us live in a horrible slum while
a few, like the United States, live on a glittering gold coast. In this

situation, the world needs prophetic leaders who can meet people where they are, but also meet them where they are not. Leaders have the difficult task of helping to change false perceptions and simplistic thinking.

Relief, Development or Public Policy Advocacy?

The American people, then, pride themselves on their compassion toward people who are in trouble because of some catastrophe beyond their control. American churches and their subsidiary organizations have been exemplary in programs of relief and rehabilitation aimed at meeting tragic human need. They have helped move the American government to action, while working directly with those who suffer as victims.

The churches are to be applauded for this compassion and service as an act of charity. It represents the impulse of Christ who fed the multitude when his followers were without food.

Three historical strands are converging now to increase the churches' involvement in development projects. First, they are evolving from the soil of the foreign mission movement. Today, many churches specify that projects must originate among indiginous churches or be recommended by missionaries. Secondly, development projects emerge from relief and rehabilitation programs and follow as a logical next step. Finally, since 1973 the churches have become directly involved in foreign aid programs through contract with AID. They have seen first hand the need and the potential for good in development projects. They have also recognized the advanatages, in may cases, of working independently of AID is small-scale projects that meet human need more creatively and with less red tape.

The total expenditure of church funds by American denominations in mission work, relief, rehabilitation and development may reach a billion dollars this year. That is a significant commitment, and several million persons will be affected, most of them positively, by this effort on the part of the churches.

But the question persists: Can the churches be content to work directly for the benefit of even fifty million persons, when there are or five hundred million people in total poverty, malnourished, and hovering on the brink of starvation?

The answer is not an "either-or" but a "both-and." Those who work in current programs should in no way apologize, nor should this work be diminished. BUT IT IS NO SUBSTITUTE FOR BENDING EVERY EFFORT TO BUILD A MORE JUST INTERNATIONAL ORDER. That is the more critical task because it affects by far the most people.

III. CHANGING THE BASIC GLOBAL SYSTEM VS. STRUCTURAL CHANGES WITHIN NATIONS

When one begins with the question, "What is keeping people poor and hungry?" the perceptive observer looks to systemic causes. First, the global economic system is structured to favor the rich and oppress the poor, and many developing nations are structured to maintain the political power and economic ascendancy of people locked into their positions of poverty.

Which one of these powerful obstacles to global justice should be the focus of attention in the strategy of the churches? Again, this is a "both-and" situation and not an "either-or." Most of the church-sponsored public policy programs (Interreligious Task Force on U.S. Food Policy, and Bread for the World) today place the emphasis on the latter. Bread for the World, for example, has an imaginative legislative agenda. It is trying to get changes in Title I of the PL-480 Program which require distribution of food in a more equitable manner. Pressure is being applied on Congress to force AID to provide more aid to countries that better distribute the benefits within their economies, so that the poor benefit directly and not just indirectly. As part of their major legislative program, "BREAD" asks the United States to lobby the World Bank to give at least half of their loans to projects that benefit directly the poorest members within nations where the loans are made.

There is a fine line between recognizing the sovereignty of independent nations and, on the other hand, using the carrot and stick to encourage these nations to develop more humane economic policies. So long as that line is not crossed, it is legitimate to favor those nations which help the poor the most. However, the process becomes somewhat suspect and even hypocritical when our righteous indignation is directed toward the policies of other countries, and when these rulers learned about inequity from the powerful industrial nations.

Do rich landlords make large profits from the labor of poorly paid landless peasants? Yes, but do rich countries make policies that keep poor countries in servitude? The average American income is more than $9,000 per year; the average income per person in developing nations is $300 per year.

One recalls the powerful sermon of the prophet Amos as recorded in the first chapter of the book that bears his name. First, Amos denounced the crimes of Damascus, then those of the Philistines in Gaza. Next in order were those of Tyre, Edom, Ammon and Moab. The people of Judah listened enraptured to the good sermon of Amos as he pronounced God's judgment on their sins. But then Amos turned to Israel and said that despite God's special favor, they, too, were guilty. Corruption and luxury for some at the expense of others were chief sins of Israel. Amos could only reach the conclusion that God would condemn their actions as much as those of the other nations.

Since the U.S. has more power to control its own policies than those of other nations, and since the centerpiece of injustice is the international economic order itself, it would seem appropriate to make this issue central in the struggle against world hunger. If we support economic policies that expand trade, stabilize prices, reduce inflation, and if we bring developing nations into the mainstream of the global economy, then we will have set an example. From that base we will be in a better position to put pressure on internal practices of other nations. Further, if the total economic pie of the world is enlarged and more goes to each struggling nation, there is a chance that they will distribute the income in ways that will increasingly benefit their citizens. But unless that pie is expanded there is no chance that the poorest and most hungry will have basic human needs met.

Because of this bias, the analysis of the first chapter focused more on international institutions and global systems and the role of the United States in them than it did on changing the structures within developing nations. There is no sense of regret for trying to influence internal structures of other nations if at the same time, equal or greater emphasis is being placed on a healthy, viable and just international economic order.

IV. A BOLD, IMAGINATIVE PROGRAM OF ACTION

The Bible begins with a vision of paradise, a garden of plenty. After Adam and Eve are driven from their home because of sin, humankind, still made in the image of God, is caught in the vise of sin. This is the chronicle of human history depicted in the Old Testament.

Then came the Christ, who through his life, death and resurrection broke the power of sin and death. The "good news" is that we live now in the power of the resurrection. The decisive battle has been won, even though the war against principalities and the powers of evil still rages.

In the Book of Revelation, we catch the vision of a new garden of plenty -- where the trees of life grow along the river that flows to the throne of God and where "the leaves of the trees are for the healing of the nations."

We are keenly aware of the continuing power of sin and death. This power seems to be growing so that an ultimate point might be reached in which the world will experience a rain of missiles and bombs with the potential to end human life on the planet. Conversely, if Christ is lifted up and people are drawn to him -- to his compassion and caring -- then the power is present to help answer the prayer taught to us by the Lord, "Thy kingdom come, thy will be done, on earth as it is in heaven." The technical capacity is at hand either to destroy the planet and its people or to build a garden of plenty for all members of the family of God. While we can never equate the kingdom of God with a world without poverty, we can say that His kingdom on earth is not one where a few people live in luxury and hundreds of millions of others must deny their essential personhood because of hunger and malnourishment.

At this time, when one-eighth of the earth's people have total incomes of $200 per year or less, the church could hold an incarnational theology where Christ comes to earth again through his church. Not only is there ministry to the poor; the oppression of all modern Pharoahs is also broken, as these 500 million people march through the Red Sea toward a new promised land of basic human decency.

The blueprint for how this can be done is contained essentially in in the books <u>North-South: A Program for Survival</u> and <u>Overcoming World Hunger: The Challenge Ahead.</u>

The unique role of the church is first and foremost to hold by faith a strong positive vision of both the justice of God and the love of God. The church, however, will not be content to be isolated from the world it is called to serve. The implication of the vision is that Christians will also enter the incarnational experience by involving themselves in the world of political debate, policy formulation and strategy sessions. Informed Christians across the country can become involved and on the alert to exercise their vote and influence as citizens. They will rejoice in victory as new public policies are adopted that change fundamental structures in favor of the oppressed of the earth.

Let us move from reflection on the great realities of our faith to some specific suggestions as to ingredients which are needed to implement this vision.

Employ and Help Finance Scholars

The churches need the services of persons who are at home in both theology and international economics to help analyze the structures of the global economy and show where and how changes can be made with minimal harm in the process. The churches today employ thousands of persons in world missions, in relief and rehabilitation projects, and in small-scale church-sponsored development programs. Only a handful are employed to work at the level of public policy formulation or to lobby for enactment of legislation favored by them. And <u>almost nobody</u> is employed to do the work of research and reflection that is so much needed to help the churches formulate the most productive public policy positions. Without this assistance, many well-intentioned policy groups tend to major on minors or they lack the hard information they need to be most effective in the high-stakes game of getting legislation adopted. A bold program of action will begin by spending money to employ competent scholars.

Utilize Expert Laypersons in the Churches

As a way of partially remedying the dearth of scholarship at the command of the churches and as a way of taking seriously the "priesthood of all believers," the churches would do well to actively ferret out scholars in the universities, the think-tanks, the labor unions, the corporations, and in the government, who are experts and who are Christians -- lay members of these same churches. This cadre of unused or under-used talent waits an invitation to join the bold exploration of how they can be co-creators with God, and servants of His Christ in helping to form the new world order that is free from hunger.

Brainstorm Creative Proposals

In studying the hunger programs of the denominations and those of interdenominational groups, one finds that almost everything being said or proposed is useful. Most emphasis is on issues that will be helpful but may not be central to the larger vision of a world without hunger. But most of what is proposed is second-handed, and is often in response to what is already being done or proposed by others. The denominational executives are busy with administrative chores, and there are few scholars working for the churches. The ingredients are not present for journeys to the mountains where people dream and plan and find breakthroughs to current stalemates. Yet this ministry is one of the most important that could be performed by the churches. The bold program of action will unfold only after a great deal of creative brainstorming.

An Example of Creative Planning

As presented previously, Bread for the World had input into the thinking of the U.S. Treasury Department and Congresspersons in the formulation of lending policies of the Inter-American Bank. A new policy resulted in which 50 percent of all loans now go to projects that directly benefit those in absolute poverty. BREAD is now urging the Congress to use its influence with the World Bank to adopt the same policy. With $16 to $20 billion being loaned to developing counties each year for the next several years, the impact for good on the poorest people would be truly significant if the policy is enacted.

A New Mode of Thinking: Taxes on International Transactions

The mind can soar into the blue skies when the window is opened to the possibility of taxing international transactions for the benefit of poor nations. Within enlightened nation states, of course, that is exactly what happens: taxes are levied, and part of the revenue is used to support and supplement the poor.

The ability to levy taxes will be an inevitable step as world government emerges. The acceptance of taxation as a source of revenue and as a means of transferring wealth from rich to poor nations is a profoundly important step. While it may seem revolutionary to some, it is an obvious next step in the thinking of others. First proposed by Barbara Ward, the concept can be discussed, developed and shared widely. Some possibilities for taxation are:

(a) Ocean Mining and Fishing

Arvid Pardo, Ambassador of Malta to the United Nations, made the initial proposal for a "Law of the Sea" Conference to establish a system of international law to govern use of the oceans. As part of his plan he suggested the use of profits from mining in the oceans as a special fund for development. Manganese nodules and other minerals on the ocean floor cannot be mined until there is a final decision on this controversial aspect of the Law of the Sea Treaty. To get acceptance of this provision would open the door to the principle of using the common heritage of mankind for the common good of mankind. Oil deposits in the oceans beyond the territorial limits of any country offer an additional legitimate possibility for revenue for United Nations programs to eliminate poverty. Others have suggested a tax on all commercial fishing in the oceans beyond territorial waters of nations.

(b) Tax on Shipment of Goods and Commodities

Another proposal that merits special attention is to charge a tax on grain purchases from one developed nation to another. The funds gathered from this tax might go to supplement the purchase price of additional grain for the poorest countries. A similar charge might be considered on both commodities and manufactured goods flowing from one developed nation to another.

(c) Communication and Transportation Fees

There is a ready rationale for a tax on international air transportation since oxygen, the common property of mankind, is used in large amounts by every jet airplane. Other fees could be levied on international communications systems and satellites in outer space. A similar tax would be appropriate for the transport of goods by ship across international waterways.

(d) Surcharge on Sale of Armaments

Tucked away in this list is a proposed surcharge to be levied on the sale of international armaments. As many countries now try to discourage the sale of cigarettes by placing a heavy tax on them, so might a high tax be the occasion for discouraging sale of armaments. At the current rate of arms purchase, a ten percent tax would provide more development assistance or capital for economic growth than any other funding source in the world.

The Liberation of the Churches

Church leaders, like all persons who lead large groups of people, must be concerned about the reaction of their constituents. How do church leaders get the people in the pews to lend support rather than express skepticism or outright hostility?

There are many types of leadership. Church leaders may feel they must wait until people are ready, and so shut out near-term consideration of global injustice. They may take a "go slow" approach, drop hints, but go no further. Others will decide to act, but will do so quietly and without stirring opposition. Another style is to set forth a total agenda, but place emphasis on those parts where there is most agreement, with the hope of gradually moving into areas where differences are greatest.

Perhaps what is needed now is a bolder leader -- one who sets forth a challenging agenda and shows without apology why it is important. This leader will express respect for those who disagree, but will act with awareness of those who are victims of injustice. She/he asserts the issues as they are -- life and death matters for hundreds of millions of people.

Such a bold and forthright position may mean the salvation of the church. Jesus' said that many good people will be surprised to find themselves outside the Kingdom, while others are unexpectedly admitted. The criterion for entry: "I was hungry and you gave me food...thirsty and you gave me to drink." We can never hope to enter the Kingdom until we bring others with us. Such a leader will seek to rouse the slumbering church with this new priority. Such a leader will not wait while millions of people are losing their essential humanity.

It is easier for the armchair prophet to prescribe than for church leaders to risk their own jobs. Those who care about the harmony and viability of their own religious groups do not want to advocate a policy that will create division if it can be avoided. Yet the justification for this study is, in part, to permit an independent observer to speak the prophetic word.

At this time many American churches are inhibited by persons like Dr. Ernest Lefever who criticize their social vision as "naive" or "romantic." He ridicules the churches for seeing world poverty not as a "condition" but as a "problem." Church leaders who are keenly aware of the growing power of the new right and the vast sums of money they raise have been thrown on the defensive while the Moral Majority-types speak with bold confidence.

The church needs, more than anything else, its own liberation. When leaders speak boldly in the name of a compassionate Christ and share a vision of a common humanity, they can shed their temerity and walk in the power of the resurrection. When that happens the uncertain trumpet is no longer sounded and the soldiers of the cross gird themselves for the battle.

V. SIX HUNCHES BASED ON A STUDY OF THE CHURCHES' HUNGER PROGRAMS

1. Each church faces the same basic dilemma: relief and rehabilitation programs need to raise money, which is given generously until the focus moves to public policy and the need to restructure the international economic order. As a result, church leaders hedge, apologize, and skirt the underlying issues in order to keep their programs vital and viable.

2. Educational materials produced by the denominations are not adequate for the need. All hunger programs -- and all denominational leaders -- recognize the importance of educating the people in the pews, but they are not taking the next steps and developing coherent and thorough educational materials. Educators who are knowledgeable about hunger are spread through the various bureaus, and their materials seldom get coordinated or used effectively.

3. The churches are good at "promotion" -- setting up special program emphases. Special staff persons are chosen, as in the case of world hunger programs, and then the special projects tend to operate almost independently of the regular structures of the denominations or of the National Council of Churches. This process has the advantage of providing new projects with relative freedom and the ability to mount them quickly, but the disadvan-

tage is that older bureaus are influenced in a limited way. New priorities seldom change traditional structures.

4. Some of the best work in the area of world hunger is done in organizations supported by the churches, with some distance from denominational control. For example, Bread for the World appeals to evangelicals, mainstream Protestants, and Roman Catholics, yet is free to take positions independent of any of them. The Interrelilgious Task Force has denominational representatives on its policy panels, but acts independently while representing denominational positions.

5. The denominational staffs at the United Nations seldom have contact with world hunger staff members of the same denominations. Since there is little contact, there are fewer attempts at cooperative strategic planning or to implement public policy based on the insights of hunger specialists.

6. The vigor with which "hunger programs" are promoted within the churches is waning, although a high level of support can be sustained for several years.

VI. TEN IMPERTINENT SUGGESTIONS FOR CHURCH LEADERS

1. While not needing to support every proposal of the Group of 77, churches might consider supporting the drive for a new international economic order as a way to align themselves with God's demand for justice. Fair prices for commodities might be presented in terms of the South's need for parity; e.g., for their commodities to be worth as much as they were during a specified time in terms of what they will purchase.

2. Church-related hunger programs might consider giving much stronger emphasis to the crux of the issue -- to injustice in the structures of the international political economy. The churches would demonstrate their seriousness by organizing a new lobby on trade policies and monetary issues in the context of the United Nations.

3. Existing church-related public policy groups may want to concentrate more attention on U. S. policy in the United Nations and its specialized agencies, and on administrative policies within U.S. Government Departments, while continuing to monitor and lobby Congress.

4. Church hunger programs may wish to keep clear in their education programs the correlation between military expenditures and world poverty. A phased de-escalation in the Soviet-American arms race could become the model for arms limitation and control in other parts of the world. Church literature might point out how hard it is to think of people "out there" as real persons who are hungry, while we are exporting arms for their destruction.

5. The agenda for eliminating world hunger presented in the book North-South: A Program for Survival is comprehensive and realistic. The churches might consider sponsoring nationwide educational programs designed to

help constituents understand this book as a practical guide for overcoming world hunger by the year 2000. (It should be noted that this book is a best seller in Great Britain and throughout much of Europe.)

6. As every industrialized nation has special programs that provide food for the hungry, basic assistance for those in special need, and economic opportunity for the disadvantaged, the churches might now consider sounding a call for the world community to assume this responsibility for all of its citizens. A global grain reserve program will be a permanent feature of any interdependent food system; a world food stamp program might be advocated until world hunger has completely been eliminated through other methods.

7. The churches may wish to advocate the imposition of a United Nations tax on all international trade, international transportation by air or water, on deep-sea mining, and on the sale of international arms, to provide financing for the entire agenda of eliminating poverty and hunger.

8. The churches of the United States may wish to work with other churches worldwide to promote a food stamp program open to all malnourished people of the world. It is suggested that this global project be financed as follows: (a) 25 percent from a tax on international sale of grain between first and second world countries; (b) 25 percent from PL-480, along with a similar program from other major grain-producing countries; (c) 25 percent from the International Monetary Fund; and (d) 25 percent from the host government. Alternately, this last money would be supplied by voluntary contributions from churches and other private philanthropic groups worldwide on condition that the host government use the money for projects that increase food production to serve the needs of the poor in the host countries.

9. The churches might sponsor a coordinated and greatly expanded national emphasis on systemic causes underlying world hunger, models for development and the need for a new international economic order. The program might be modeled after Canada's Ten Great Days of Sharing or Great Britain's Christian Aid Emphasis. Church World Service might assume the leadership role for Protestants with the suggestion that funds for education be increased from .5 to 10-15 percent of the annual budget.

10. Bread, which is basic to our humanity, may be the medium for finally expressing the unity of our faith. Protestant denominations, Roman Catholics and Jews might convene an unprecedented assembly for 30-50 leaders of each body to pray, study, make personal commitments, and plan how they can mobilize within the United States and with Christians and other religious bodies worldwide, to undertake with single-minded devotion the task of eliminating the scourge of hunger from planet earth.

FOOTNOTES

Chapter 1: Toward the Elimination of World Hunger

1. U.S. General Accounting Office, World Hunger: Implications for U.S. Policies (Washington, D.C.: 1979).

2. Bread for the World, "Background Paper No. 4" (New York: 1975).

3. Overcoming World Hunger: The Challenge Ahead, Report of the Presidential Commission on World Hunger. U.S. Government Printing Office, (Washington, D.C.: March 1980), pp. 8-12.

4. Ibid., p. 16.

5. North-South: A Program for Survival (Cambridge, Mass.: The MIT Press, October 1980), p. 55.

6. Erik Eckholm, Worldwatch, Paper 9, Washington, D.C.: 1976).

7. Brandt, North-South, p. 78.

8. Francis Moore Lappe' and Joseph Collins, Food First, Institute for Food and Development Policy (Boston: Mifflin Company, 1977), p. 13.

9. Lester R. Brown, World Without Borders (New York: Vintage Books, 1973), p. 85.

10. Overcoming World Hunger: The Challenge Ahead, p. 33.

11. Identifying a Food Policy Agenda for the 1980s: A Working Paper, Interreligious Task Force on U.S. Food Policy. (Washington, D.C.: January 1980).

12. Overcoming World Hunger: The Challenge Ahead, p. 29.

13. Brandt, North-South, p. 32.

14. Ibid., p. 58.

15. The emphasis in many hunger organizations at this time is to focus on inequity within nations rather than deal directly with the global economic system.

16. Interview with Tim Atwater, Research Director on International Economics, Interreligious Task Force on U.S. Food Policy. August 3, 1981.

17. Overcoming World Hunger: The Challenge Ahead, p. 3.

18. Ibid., p. 11.

19. Brandt, <u>North-South</u>, p. 29.

20. Ibid., pp. 64-65.

21. Tom Hanks, Professor of Old Testament, Seminario Biblico-Latin Americano, San Jose, Costa Rica, <u>Sojourners</u>, "Why People Are Poor" (Washington, D.C.: January 1981).

22. Ibid.

23. J. Philip Wogaman, "The Just Society in Christian Perspective." Prepared for the working group on Political Economy, Churches' Center for Theology and Public Policy, (Washington, D.C.: March 1981).

24. <u>Overcoming World Hunger: The Challenge Ahead</u>, p. 30.

25. Ibid., p. 31.

26. Brandt, <u>North-South</u>, p. 11.

27. <u>Development and International Cooperation</u>, (New York: 1976), p. 6.

28. <u>HUNGER</u>, No. 25. Published by the Interreligious Task Force on U.S. Food Policy, (Washington, D.C.: November 1980).

29. <u>Washington Post</u>, by David B. Ottaway, September 19, 1980.

30. <u>Washington Post</u>, "Ministers Finish Plans for North-South Summit" by Don Oberdorfer, August 3, 1981.

31. <u>New York Times</u>, by Bernard D. Nossiter, August 7, 1981.

32. <u>Washington Post</u>, August 11, 1981.

33. This study was concluded on September 2, 1981, and therefore does not provide information on the outcome of the Conference at Cancun.

34. <u>Washington Post</u>, "Paris' Policy Increasingly at Odds with U.S." by Edward Cody, September 2, 1981.

35. Brandt, <u>North-South</u>, p. 142.

36. <u>Washington Post</u>, "Niger Boosts Food Production Under Tough Military Rule" by Leon Dash, March 16, 1981.

37. Brandt, <u>North-South</u>, p. 150.

38. <u>New York Times</u>, by Bernard D. Nossiter, August 7, 1981.

39. Monetarism is a school of economics which wishes to control the size and rate of increase of the supply of money as the primary tool of economic management.

40. Much of this discussion was taken from HUNGER, No. 22, February 1980.

41. Some administration officials have set out to restore the gold standard.

42. Washington Post, by Ward Sinclair, July 24, 1981.

43. This report is taken from Global Negotiation Action Notes, The Global Negotiations Action Project, New York. No. 14, June 22, 1981.

44. Brandt, North-South, P. 251.

45. Overcoming World Hunger: The Challenge Ahead, pp. 108-149.

46. Jack Nelson, Hunger for Justice, Orbis Books. (Maryknoll, New York: 1980), p. 16.

47. Ibid., pp. 24-25.

48. Hunger, "Multinational Corporations and Global Development" published by IMPACT, No. 24, (Washington, D.C.: July 1980).

49. Ibid.

50. Washington Post, by Rowland Evans and Robert Novak, August 17, 1981.

51. Washington Post, by Theo Sommer, editor of Die Zeit, August 17, 1981.

52. Ruth Leger Sword, World Military and Social Expenditures 1980, World priorities, (Leesburg, Virginia 1980).

53. Alan Geyer, The Military Market: Arms Exports in Christian Perspective. A study document of the National Council of Churches, (New York: 1978), pp. 16-17.

Chapter 2: The Churches and World Hunger Since 1974

1. Leading a World of Change, United Nations Association of the USA, (New York: 1980).

2. Overcoming World Hunger: The Challenge Ahead, p.65.

3. Gustavo Gutierrez, A Theology of Liberation, translated and edited by Caridad Inda and John Eagleson, Orbis Books, (Maryknoll, New York: 1973).

4. Tracy Early, Simply Sharing, World Council of Churches, (Geneva: 1980), p. 60.

5. Ibid., p. 56.

6. An eye witness account by Edward Snyder, September 19, 1979, as reported in HUNGER, No. 21. Published by IMPACT, December 1979.

7. Many Earle, The Crisis in East Africa, The Hunger Project, (Washington, D.C.: 1981).

Chapter 3:   A Critical Review of Church-Related Hunger Programs

1.   The Methodist Church, General Conference, 1980.

2.   Global Negotiations Action Notes, No. 19, August 31, 1981.

3.   Presented by Joseph Gremillion, Orbis Books, (Maryknoll, New York: 1976).

4.   Interview with Reverend J. Bryan Hehir, August 2, 1981.

5.   J. Bryan Hehir, testimony before the Foreign Relations Committee, U.S. Senate, May 12, 1981.

6.   From the pamphlet, Focus: Toward a World That Is Human.

7.   Issue Number 40.

8.   Holy Cross and World Hunger, published by Society of Holy Cross, (Notre Dame, Indiana: 1978), p. 90.

9.   John V. Taylor, Enough is Enough, Student Christian Movement Press, London: 1975).

10.   Letter from Robert McClean to Robert McCan, dated August 5, 1981.

11.   In the PCUS, the General Assembly serves as its highest court.   There are 400 commissioners, half clergy and half laity.   Each Assembly speaks for itself, but its pronouncements are official positions of the church until they are changed.

12.   Minutes of the General Assembly, 1973.   "A Report to the 113th General Assembly from the Task Force on World Hunger," pp. 204-205.

13.   Arthur and Paul Simons, The Politics of World Hunger, Harper's Magazine Press, (New York: 1973).

14.   Background Paper #45, April, 1980.

15.   Identifying a Food Policy Agenda for the 1980s: A Working Paper, (Washington, D.C., 1980).

16.   Ibid., pp. 12-17.

17.   A brochure, A New Look, A Continuing Story, Church World Service.

18.   June 3-4, 1981.

19.   Daniel L. Force, Crop Constituency Education Pilot Program, (Elkhart, Indiana: 1979).

20.   Robert E. Ward, National Needs for International Education, Georgetown University, 1977.

21.   Frances Moore Lappe' and William Valentine, What Can We Do?. Food and Hunger, How you can make a difference, Institute for Food and Development Policy, (San Francisco: 1980), pp. 4-6.

Chapter 4: An Evaluation of the Churches' Response -- with Suggestions

1. Parts of this discussion were taken from the Constituency Education Pilot Program of CROP.

2. Overcoming World Hunger: The Challenge Ahead, p. 122.

3. Wall Street Journal, July 17, 1975.